A FAITH BUILT ON

SAND

*The Foolishness of Popular
Religion in a Postmodern Age*

A FAITH BUILT ON SAND

The Foolishness of Popular Religion in a Postmodern Age

PHIL SANDERS

From the Speaker of *In Search of the Lord's Way*

Gospel Advocate Company
Nashville, Tennessee

OTHER BOOKS BY PHIL SANDERS

Adrift

You Don't Have to Worry

Let All the Earth Keep Silence

Evangelism Handbook of New Testament Christianity

Published by Gospel Advocate Co.
1006 Elm Hill Pike, Nashville, TN 37210
www.gospeladvocate.com

ISBN 10: 0-89225-579-X
ISBN 13: 978-0-89225-579-5

DEDICATION

To my beloved wife, Jackie, my dear companion and the love of my life, I dedicate this book. When the Lord brought her into my life, He did so to bless me and help me. No husband could be more blessed than to have such a wise and faithful wife.

5

TABLE OF CONTENTS

FOREWORD   9

PREFACE   11

CHAPTER 1   *A Faith for All*   15

CHAPTER 2   *The Living and Abiding Word*   25

CHAPTER 3   *Culture and Christianity*   33

CHAPTER 4   *Cultural Morality*   43

CHAPTER 5   *Playing Church*   55

CHAPTER 6   *The Newly Defined Tolerance*   67

CHAPTER 7   *Bullied by Perceptions*   79

CHAPTER 8   *The Vanishing of Heresy*   89

CHAPTER 9   *The Emerging Church*   105

CHAPTER 10   *Synthetic Christianity*   119

CHAPTER 11   *Popular Religion*   131

CHAPTER 12   *Who Is My Brother?*   143

CHAPTER 13   *Back to the Cross*   155

ENDNOTES   167

ETERNAL TRUTH
in an Uncertain Age

The Gospel Advocate Co. has a long history of service to the Lord's church. Consistently, since 1855, its publications have featured a wide range of talented writers and have addressed the relevant issues facing Christians in each generation.

One of the significant authors contributing to this dialogue of faith is Phil Sanders. Through many articles, Phil has ably spoken to a broad scope of issues. However, his most notable contribution in publication has been his book *Adrift*.

Drawing from his graduate training in apologetics and from his astute observations as an evangelist, Phil provided the churches of Christ with a thorough explanation of trends in society as they challenge and influence Christian faith. *Adrift* was, and is, an essential reference for every church leader and for every concerned Christian. *A Faith Built on Sand* is a continuation of this discussion and provides an update of the continued challenges brought by current influences affecting the Lord's church.

Phil begins this study with an explanation of God's universal truth revealed in Jesus Christ. This message is one of hope and of despair. For those who receive the truth in obedient faith, there is the assurance of eternal life. For those who reject the truth in disbelief, there is the assurance of everlasting death. The standard of judgment is universal, and that standard is set by God alone.

In subsequent chapters, *A Faith Built on Sand* provides a detailed explanation of various ways error conflicts with God's universal truth, and it offers an explanation of how faithful Christians can resist this challenge. Finally, Phil closes by returning to the first principles of the gospel. The cross of Christ provides a perfect answer to the questions facing Christians in each generation.

As you read this book, you may find Phil's message disturbing. If so, then you have gotten the point. The churches of Christ are poised between two paths. On the one hand is the narrow way of obedient faith. On the other is the broad way of cultural accommodation. Although one way leads to eternal life, the other ends with eternal destruction. If you are not troubled with the prospect of Christians losing their faith, then you do not grasp the reality of the current crisis.

Phil, however, keeps the pioneer optimism of his native Oklahoma. His message is not one of despair, but of hope. Phil does not merely expose the danger of error; he provides clear guidance as to how the Lord's church can regain the spiritual vigor that comes only through the power of hearing and obeying the Word of God. In the grace of God revealed in Scripture, Phil shows us God's promise for the future and God's blessing for the church today.

I believe this book will bless the Lord's work in many ways. Elders in congregations will find in *A Faith Built on Sand* wise counsel to help them properly guide the flock of God in their care. Preachers and Bible class teachers will find much material in this book useful in preparing lessons that address the central needs of the church today. As faithful Christians consider Phil's message, they all will strengthen their resolve to press on in the way of truth.

With gratitude for the intellect but more importantly for the conviction that Phil brought in writing this book, I recommend it to God's people as a useful tool in the Lord's service.

Gregory Alan Tidwell
Minister, Columbus, Ohio

PREFACE

For everyone who does wicked things hates the light and
does not come to the light, lest his deeds should be exposed
(John 3:20). Submit yourselves therefore to God. Resist the
devil, and he will flee from you (James 4:7).

No matter how many people steal, stealing remains wrong.
No matter how many people are corrupt, corruption remains
wrong. No matter how many people betray public trust, that
action remains wrong. The fact that any misdeed becomes
popular does not make it permissible. The problem of evil
is not solved by multiplication. – Sidney Greenberg[1]

Siblings can differ greatly. The twin sons of Isaac and Rebekah, Esau
and Jacob, differed greatly in their desires and outlooks on life; yet
they came from the same father and mother. Early in life they lived in
the same tent, heard the same stories of their father and grandfather,
and ate the same food. Yet they looked and spoke differently. One was
hairy and the other smooth, and Isaac, although aged and blind, could
still distinguish the voice of Esau from the voice of Jacob.

Differences do not change parentage. With all our disparities and diversity, we are still the children of God the Father. He is the "Father of spirits" (Hebrews 12:9). He is the Father of everyone's spirit; everyone in all places with all languages for all time. Paul proclaimed at Mars Hill that God

made from one man every nation of mankind to live on all the face of the earth, having determined allotted periods and the boundaries of their dwelling place, that they should seek God, in the hope that they might feel their way toward him and find him. Yet he is actually not far from each one of us, for "In him we live and move and have our being"; as even some of your own poets have said, "For we are indeed his offspring" (Acts 17:26-28).

He created each one and will judge each one. He commands all men everywhere to repent. We are all accountable to the Lord. We are accountable whether we know it, whether we acknowledge it, or whether we agree to it.

For the word of God is living and active, sharper than any two-edged sword, piercing to the division of soul and of spirit, of joints and of marrow, and discerning the thoughts and intentions of the heart. And no creature is hidden from his sight, but all are naked and exposed to the eyes of him to whom we must give account (Hebrews 4:12-13).

Time and distance do not erase accountability. A change in the winds of cultural worldview does not release anyone from God's jurisdiction. We are accountable to Him in matters large and small.

The covenant of Jesus Christ has been open to all people since the day of Pentecost; "the grace of God has appeared, bringing salvation for all people" (Titus 2:11). Jesus is Lord of all, and "in every nation anyone who fears him and does what is right is acceptable to him" (Acts 10:35-36). We cannot hope to enjoy the blessings of salvation apart from commitment to the Lord. If the blessing is offered to all, so is the accountability. Covenants come with blessings and responsibilities, and the covenant of Christ is no less. Although everyone can call Jesus "Lord," those who will not do His will speak in vain. "Not everyone who says to me, 'Lord, Lord,' will enter the kingdom of heaven, but the one who does the will of my Father who is in heaven" (Matthew 7:21). Only those who do His will can hope to claim His favor and blessing. One cannot have Jesus as Savior if he does not treat Jesus as Lord.

Pointing to Jesus alone as Savior and Lord runs counter to the post-modern mind. Postmodernists are not content to let Him or any religion have power over their lives. They believe postmodern man is wiser than God, and God must be held in check to the "religiously correct" views of the day. They feel free to bully the God of the Bible with their "superior" ethic and tolerance. They feel the need to hold God accountable to the cultural mores of the day. They forget that men remain accountable to God.

If postmodernists were set adrift in the last decade by their mindset, they are well on their way to being utterly confused at the present. They know what they do not want, but what they do not want is what they most need. They are experimenting with the old and the new; they are seeking but not finding. They have nothing authentic to say because they do not know what is authentically best. They do not find because they have quit looking in the place they most need to look. They have quit listening where they most need to listen. The world will not lead them closer to the Lord; only the Word of God can do that. So with ruthless abandon they journey farther from God without realizing it. Without God, they are without hope and without real direction. They have left themselves vulnerable to whatever deception comes along. In time they will collapse under their confusion because they built their lives on a foundation of sand.

My hope in this book is to speak to the pressing issues of our day, the mindsets that destroy our faith and our hope. In this sequel to my former book *Adrift*, I want to look in the first two chapters into the foundation of our faith, realizing God's universal plan revealed in the living and abiding Word. In chapters 3-11, the reader will be able to explore the cultural changes affecting the church and how they are revealed through the new mindsets of an emerging church and popular religion. The final two chapters bring us back to the need to find what God approves and to take a long look at the cross.

With deep appreciation to many, I offer this sequel to *Adrift*. I have written it with the church in mind, hoping to help elders, ministers and brethren who love the Lord to make some sense of the vast changes taking place in society and in the religious world. No one knows everything, and I am subject to mistakes in fact or in judgment, for which I alone am responsible. I pray I have opened a discussion, however, about the most important matters of life and how we are to understand them.

My profound thanks to my dear friend Greg Tidwell not only for writing the foreword for this book but also for his enduring friendship and encouragement. Greg encouraged me in the writing of *Adrift* and encouraged me all the more in this book. He is a trusted brother and a fellow soldier for the cause of Christ. Without his help and wisdom, I would be much poorer indeed.

I am grateful to my mentors William Jones of Oklahoma Christian University, Jimmy Jividen, Cecil May, Tom Holland and Neil Anderson. These precious men have helped to shape my life.

I am grateful to my co-workers at *In Search of the Lord's Way* for their patience with me as I wrote. They have helped me greatly, and I treasure them. Thank you Mack Lyon, Chris Lyon, Craig Dodgen, Kerry Campbell, Jerry Campbell, Barbara Campbell, Donna Demos and Kendal Edmison.

To my four daughters and my sons-in-law who have helped me greatly to understand the times and to know what a Christian should do, I can only express my deepest thanks. They have patiently endured my discourses and helped me sharpen my thinking. I love each of them as God's great gift to my wife, Jackie, and me. As with my earlier book, I wrote this book with them in mind. But now, a decade later, I have several grandchildren whose futures cause me the greatest concern.

My parents, Harley and Euletta Sanders, have been such a deep source of faith and dedication in my life. Their decisions to live for the Lord led me to do the same. I treasure the memory of my father and the abiding faith of my dear mother. I am a preacher because of them. I must also recognize the memory of my father-in-law and mother-in-law, Jack and Bernice Dodgen, whose deep commitment to what is right has often refreshed my spirit and encouraged me.

CHAPTER 1

A FAITH for All

Christianity stands in stark contrast with the Judaism that preceded it. Christianity does not tie faith in God to a physical nation; rather faith in Jesus is for all people in all places for all time. "There is neither Jew nor Greek, there is neither slave nor free, there is no male and female, for you are all one in Christ Jesus" (Galatians 3:28).

God remembered the prayers of Cornelius and His promise to the Gentiles. An angel in a vision told Cornelius, "[S]end men to Joppa and bring one Simon who is called Peter. He is lodging with one Simon, a tanner, whose house is by the sea" (Acts 10:5-6).

At the same time, God had to convince Peter the gospel was for all. Until that time, the apostles preached only to Jews. Peter learned from a dramatic dream he was not to regard as common or unclean what God had now made clean (Acts 10:9-16).

The Holy Spirit directed Peter to leave Joppa for Caesarea and teach the gospel to Cornelius. Peter made the trip and found a crowd gathered to hear. He began by saying: "Truly I understand that God shows no partiality, but in every nation anyone who fears him and does what is right is acceptable to him" (Acts 10:34-35).

One Way of Salvation for All People

God loves all people everywhere.

> For God so loved the world, that he gave his only Son, that whoever believes in him should not perish but have eternal life. For God did not send his Son into the world to condemn the world, but in order that the world might be saved through him (John 3:16-17).

God showed love in sending Jesus to die for those who are weak, ungodly, sinners and enemies of the cross (Romans 5:6-10).

Because God wanted everyone to have the opportunity of salvation, Jesus gave Himself as a ransom for all people.

> This is good, and it is pleasing in the sight of God our Savior, who desires all people to be saved and to come to the knowledge of the truth. For there is one God, and there is one mediator between God and men, the man Christ Jesus, who gave himself as a ransom for all, which is the testimony given at the proper time (1 Timothy 2:3-6).

Jesus died for every person everywhere for all time.

> My little children, I am writing these things to you so that you may not sin. But if anyone does sin, we have an advocate with the Father, Jesus Christ the righteous. He is the propitiation for our sins, and not for ours only but also for the sins of the whole world (1 John 2:1-2).

Jesus tasted death for everyone (Hebrews 2:9). God has given His Son for every man, every woman, every boy and every girl. No one is excluded.

Jesus commissioned His apostles and disciples to preach the one gospel to every person in every culture, in every nation, in every language and in every age.

> All authority in heaven and on earth has been given to me. Go therefore and make disciples of all nations, baptizing them in the name of the Father and of the Son and of the Holy Spirit, teaching them to observe all that I have commanded

you. And behold, I am with you always, to the end of the age (Matthew 28:18-20).

Go into all the world and proclaim the gospel to the whole creation (Mark 16:15).

Thus it is written, that the Christ should suffer and on the third day rise from the dead, and that repentance and forgiveness of sins should be proclaimed in his name to all nations, beginning from Jerusalem (Luke 24:46-47).

Clearly, the gospel was for all people, in all ages and every culture.

One Church for All the Saved

Many early fathers referred to the church as the "catholic" church. They did not mean what has come to be the Roman Catholic Church. Instead, the word "catholic" to them meant "universal" or "worldwide." They understood that the church is universal in scope. It is not restricted to any one ethnic group or geographical location but is open to Jew and Greek, slave and free, male and female, with its gospel message directed to all nations (Galatians 3:28).

The Lord calls all people to repent. No one can ignore this call with impunity.

The times of ignorance God overlooked, but now he commands all people everywhere to repent, because he has fixed a day on which he will judge the world in righteousness by a man whom he has appointed; and of this he has given assurance to all by raising him from the dead (Acts 17:30-31).

The Lord is not slow to fulfill his promise as some count slowness, but is patient toward you, not wishing that any should perish, but that all should reach repentance (2 Peter 3:9).

No generation could exempt itself from accountability to Jesus. No generation could tell God to leave them alone. Although generations in the past abandoned God's way to follow their ways, in every case that course led to destruction. The history of idolatry in Israel shows us that popular opinions do not turn wrong into right. When Israel despised God's statutes, embraced idolatry to be like nations around them, and abandoned the commandments of God, they found out they could not dismiss God so easily. God exiled them (2 Kings 17:14-18).

Jesus Christ is Lord of all. God gave all authority to Him over every nation and culture in every age. The Father has given all things into the hands of the Son (John 3:35). Jesus prayed,

> Father, the hour has come; glorify your Son that the Son may glorify you, since you have given him authority over all flesh, to give eternal life to all whom you have given him (John 17:1-2).

> And no creature is hidden from his sight, but all are naked and exposed to the eyes of him to whom we must give account (Hebrews 4:13).

One Day of Judgment for All People

At the end of time, all nations will gather before the throne of Christ.

> When the Son of Man comes in his glory, and all the angels with him, then he will sit on his glorious throne. Before him will be gathered all the nations, and he will separate people one from another as a shepherd separates the sheep from the goats (Matthew 25:31-32).

John further explained:

> And I saw the dead, great and small, standing before the throne, and books were opened. Then another book was opened, which is the book of life. And the dead were judged by what was written in the books, according to what they had done. And the sea gave up the dead who were in it, Death and Hades gave up the dead who were in them, and they were judged, each one of them, according to what they had done (Revelation 20:12-13).

The universal character of the cross, the gospel, repentance, the church and the judgment permeates the Scriptures. The Lord of all flesh reigns over all creation (John 17:2); there is no exception.

God has highly exalted him and bestowed on him the name that is above every name, so that at the name of Jesus every knee should bow, in heaven and on earth and under the earth, and every tongue confess that Jesus Christ is Lord, to the glory of God the Father (Philippians 2:9-11).

He is the image of the invisible God, the firstborn of all creation. For by him all things were created, in heaven and on earth, visible and invisible, whether thrones or dominions or rulers or authorities – all things were created through him and for him. And he is before all things, and in him all things hold together (Colossians 1:15-17).

The Creator of all is Lord of all and Judge of all. Neither culture nor language nor education changes Him from Lord of all to fellow-religionist. The presence of other religions does not demote Him into one of many. No other is like Him; there is only one Lord (Ephesians 4:5). Christianity is not one choice in many but the only alternative. A person cannot choose his creator; he may choose in whom he will believe, but he cannot choose who made him. Nor can a person choose his eternal judge. Jesus will judge everyone, whether anyone objects or not. The presence of many world religions does not change who is my creator or my judge. Jesus is both Lord of creation and Judge of all people, and nothing can change that. One may deny it, complain about it, ignore it or dismiss it, but he cannot remove Jesus as Lord and Judge.

Such dogmatic statements about the uniqueness of Jesus seem arrogant and judgmental in our current culture, but we have more to consider than cultural opinions. Many people are quick to regard Christians as mean-spirited and negative because they do not accept everyone as equals. There is, however, no equal to Jesus Christ. Facts do not change simply because they are unfashionable.

Postmodern Confusion

Postmodernism is not a distinct set of doctrines or truth claims but (1) a mood, a view of the world characterized by a deep distrust of reason, not to mention a disdain for the knowledge Christians believe the Bible provides; and (2) a methodology, a completely new way of analyzing ideas. As a movement, postmodernism poses a fresh onslaught on truth that brings a more or less cohesive approach to literature, history, politics, education, law, sociology, linguistics and virtually every other discipline, including science. Postmodernism calls for a metamorphosis, transforming every area of life.

But postmodernists are quick to judge without realizing it. They speak with prejudice, having bought into the presuppositions of current thinking. They do not know they are displaying the narrow-mindedness they condemn. Postmodern thinkers can also be partisan and reactionary, not understanding and tolerant. They seem strangely blind to their dogmatism; they do not realize the contradictory nature of their assumptions. As a mindset, postmodernism is often a judgmental, knee-jerk reaction to everything that is modern and traditional. If someone in the modern era believed it, the postmodernist says it must be wrong.

Modernist thought centered on a belief in human progress and in reason as the ultimate source of authority. Some postmodernists are so ready to reject anything modern that they forget that logic, reasoning, faith and truth were present long before the modern era. In one conversation I had some years ago with a postmodernist, he was scolding me for speaking of the rules of logic and hermeneutics. He was sure these ideas grew out of rationalism. It did not occur to him that people were thinking even before the days of Jesus. Words that concern logic and reasoning can be found throughout the New Testament. In fact, the *Greek-English Lexicon of the New Testament Based on Semantic Domains* lists 122 words in the domain. These words involve "essentially the processing and manipulation of information, often leading to decision and choice." [1]

Many postmodernists associate tradition with modernism. If a practice was considered "traditional" during the period of modernism, then it should be questioned and dismissed because it is an effort to gain power over others. To them "tradition" is a blurred term, often referring to what people have normally done rather than what some have required to be done. So much of the current postmodern behavior is motivated by a desire to reject whatever has been the norm at church and in the home.

For centuries, people have entered spirited discussions and made logical arguments over matters of truth. Matthew records the spirited debates Jesus had with the Pharisees and Sadducees (Matthew 22). When Paul was in Athens, he "reasoned in the synagogue with the Jews and the devout persons and in the marketplace every day with those who happened to be there" (Acts 17:17). Luke remarked concerning Athens, "Now all the Athenians and the foreigners who lived there would spend their time in nothing except telling or hearing something new" (v. 21).

The pursuit of truth did not begin with modernists, nor did the debate whether all truth is relative begin with the modern era. Protagoras in the fifth century B.C. coined the phrase, "Man is the measure of all things: of things which are, that they are, and of things which are not, that they are not." In the writings of Plato, Socrates criticized the relativism of the sophists and Protagoras in the dialogue with Theaetetus. The statement "all is relative" is either a relative statement or an absolute one. If it is relative, then this statement does not rule out absolutes. If the statement is absolute, on the other hand, it provides an example of an absolute statement, proving that not all truths are relative.

Diluted Truth Leads to Deluded Thinking

Postmodern relativism is filled with "doublethink," a term coined by George Orwell in his novel *1984*, to describe the act of simultaneously accepting as correct two mutually contradictory beliefs. The religious pluralism of postmodern thinking, because it deconstructs all metanarratives, simultaneously regards all beliefs as equally true and valid while considering them benign and meaningless. In postmodern thinking, the intent of the author or speaker falls victim to whatever view the reader and listener wish to place on it. Opinions about truth trump what the truth is trying to say. People's opinions about Christ are the truth in a postmodern world. There is no place for context, history or evidence in trying to discover the truth. This is what makes doublethink possible in our postmodern culture.

Some forms of relativism make it impossible to believe one is in error. If there is no truth beyond an individual's belief that something is true, then an individual cannot hold his or her beliefs to be false or mistaken. When truth becomes relative to individuals, this relativizing destroys the distinction between truth and belief.

Facts are true, however, whether people believe them or not. Whether a culture accepts or rejects Jesus as Lord does not change that He is the creator and judge of all people everywhere in all time. Belief or disbelief does not establish fact or erase the truth. Fact is fact regardless of cultural perception.

Christianity is a faith for all. Jesus died for all; the gospel message is for all; and the church is open to all who believe and obey. This is no vain matter. Without its universal scope and promise, America today would have little hope or assurance. To subjugate Christianity to cultural perception is to cast men into darkness and uncertainty with little hope for ever finding truth. Paul observed:

> Now this I say and testify in the Lord, that you must no longer walk as the Gentiles do, in the futility of their minds. They are darkened in their understanding, alienated from the life of God because of the ignorance that is in them, due to their hardness of heart. They have become callous and have given themselves up to sensuality, greedy to practice every kind of impurity. But that is not the way you learned Christ! – assuming that you have heard about him and were taught in him, as the truth is in Jesus, to put off your old self, which belongs to your former manner of life and is corrupt through deceitful desires, and to be renewed in the spirit of your minds, and to put on the new self, created after the likeness of God in true righteousness and holiness (Ephesians 4:17-24).

Christ is all-encompassing and unique as Lord. Jesus is the "one Lord" and the "Lamb of God, who takes away the sin of the world" (John 1:29; Ephesians 4:5). The disciples who saw Him risen from the dead declared, "And there is salvation in no one else, for there is no other name under heaven given among men by which we must be saved" (Acts 4:12). God has reserved the unique place as "firstborn of all creation" for Christ alone (Colossians 1:15). If He is to be believed at all, one must admit Jesus was surely right when He said, "I am the way, and the truth, and the life. No one comes to the Father except through me" (John 14:6).

A national survey conducted by the Pew Forum on Religion & Public Life from July 31 to Aug. 10, 2008, among 2,905 adults found that a "majority of all American Christians (52%) think that at least some non-Christian faiths can lead to eternal life. Indeed, among Christians who believe many religions can lead to eternal life, 80% name at least one non-Christian faith that can do so." Interestingly, a majority of these Americans who identify themselves as Christians "believe people with no religious faith can also achieve eternal salvation (56%)," and "(42%) say this about atheists." [2]

If Jesus is not who He claimed to be, then there is little reason for any discussion about anything religious. We live in hopeless vanity. Postmodern Christians cannot in one breath claim Jesus is Lord and in another say He is merely one of many great teachers. The earliest Christians who witnessed His death and resurrection would have none of this futile neutrality about Christ. Their skepticism on Saturday night was answered on resurrection morning. The Lord appeared alive to them with many convincing proofs for a period of 40 days (Acts 1:1-3). So convinced were they of the truth of what they had witnessed, they sacrificed the rest of their lives to tell the story at great risk. They did not and would not take it back; they took Jesus' message to the whole world.

Cultural perceptions in foreign lands did not keep these early Christians from preaching Jesus. If they were persecuted, they moved to the next place telling the same story (Acts 8:4). Although they personally adapted to the cultures of the time, they never did so at the cost of their devotion to the law of Christ (1 Corinthians 9:19-23).

Paul changed his style as he entered a new culture, but he did not change his message. He kept saying the same things he had always said. A new culture does not demand a reinvented church. The church does not need a new theology; it needs God's eternal truths. Our 21st century still needs the message of the cross, still needs salvation from sin, still needs the hope of righteousness, and still needs the truth.

The Lord of heaven is wiser than we are. He put the truths we need in Scripture, not some dumbed-down stories for itching ears. He told us what we needed to hear, not what we wanted to hear. He did so out of love. Our present culture does not want to hear about sin, being lost or hell; but they need to hear about these things. I am finding it harder and harder to be a preacher in this new millennium. I believe it is much more difficult than when I began nearly 40 years ago. I am convinced, however, that being faithful as a steward of the manifold grace of God means that I preach "the whole counsel of God" (Acts 20:27).

Ed Dobson, in facing all the struggles of a postmodern world, observed that people-pleasing sermons did not always attract more than plain gospel messages. His attendance was actually higher for simple gospel sermons than it was for the "felt-need" sermons he was preaching on stress and forgiving your parents. He said,

> I learned a valuable lesson. I don't need to trade away forthright, biblical messages for something faddish or trendy. People have a basic spiritual hunger that only faithful biblical preaching can satisfy.[3]

Reaching our culture is more than filling church buildings with people. The preacher who feeds his people with spiritual junk food may draw a crowd early on, but he won't keep them. His back door is also open, and people starved for spiritual nourishment will find real hope elsewhere.

The gospel still works. It still reaches into the hearts of people who long to know God. People will not ultimately "feel good" about themselves until they find God's solution to their sin problems. That solution is for everyone everywhere at all times. It is a faith for all.

Questions

1. How does diluted truth lead to deluded thinking?

2. How does John 3:16 show that God's love is unconditional?

3. How does John 3:16 show that God's grace is conditional?

4. How are we tempted to compromise truth when friends and family members have embraced error?

CHAPTER 2

THE LIVING AND
Abiding Word

Having purified your souls by your obedience to the truth for a sincere brotherly love, love one another earnestly from a pure heart, since you have been born again, not of perishable seed but of imperishable, through the living and abiding word of God; for "All flesh is like grass and all its glory like the flower of grass. The grass withers, and the flower falls, but the word of the Lord remains forever." And this word is the good news that was preached to you (1 Peter 1:22-25).

Peter likely wrote these words from Rome where he spent his last years before his death. He was far removed from Jerusalem and the day of Pentecost when he preached his first gospel sermon. As a Jew, Peter wrote to "those who are elect exiles of the dispersion in Pontus, Galatia, Cappadocia, Asia, and Bithynia" (1 Peter 1:1). The word "dispersion" usually refers to Jews scattered outside Judea, but the use of the word "elect" shows Peter was referring to Christians, both Jew and Gentile.

Despite his move from Jerusalem to Rome, from Jewish culture to Roman, and from youth to maturity, Peter remained with his message. He realized there was no new message for a new culture. He understood that what he preached to them was the word of the Lord that would remain forever. Others in later centuries might seek to change the message, but Peter realized it was that same preached message he received from the Lord that brought about the divine new birth (2 Peter 1:16, 20-21). What he preached would remain God's message.

The Eternal and Universal Message

God's Word is an imperishable seed that is alive today and will remain so to the end of time. It will endure every cultural change through the ages; it cannot die or be destroyed. Many have always rejected it, but it endures. Persecutions did not stop God's Word from continuing to do its work.

People purify their souls and are born again when they are obedient to the truth found in this imperishable seed. Obedience is not self-designed. If the seed is planted to reproduce, it must come from God. Men cannot alter or redesign the seed and expect to get the same result. Many current preachers believe obedience to be heartfelt but not necessarily tied to ritual. They think if the heart is right, it matters little whether the person obeying conforms to the ritual. This idea is popular within the postmodern culture among churches of Christ because it allows for religious pluralism in what is required to become a Christian. They say, for instance, one does not have to be immersed to be baptized; he or she may substitute sprinkling or pouring and come out with the same result.

One must wonder, however, what Peter meant by obedience to the truth. Did he mean that we obey the truth we agree with? Did he mean we obey the truth we understand, even if our knowledge of it is imperfect? Did he mean that we are obeying the truth, even if we obey a manufactured tradition that rebels against the truth? Did he mean that we obey some of the truth but may ignore the rest? Did he mean that one is obeying the truth to the purifying of one's soul, even if one is substituting a sinner's prayer for baptism?

Some want the Man but not the plan. They want the love and grace but not the authority and the teaching. Obedience, however, demands some instruction to be obeyed. When you obey an instruction, you obey the person who gave it. That is how anyone obeys anything; he obeys the person or authority behind the instruction. One does what he or she is told to do. The whole idea of obeying someone but dismissing or contradicting his teaching is doublethink.

It is absurd to suppose we have obeyed the Lord when we have sidestepped the teaching or argued against what the Lord teaches. Immersion into Christ is a right thing, but immersing for the wrong purpose is still disobedience. Some denominations contradict the Bible regarding baptism when they claim one is saved before baptism. In fact, they fiercely condemn those who say baptism precedes salvation. The Scriptures teach that God saves through the blood of Christ at the time one is baptized (Acts 22:16; Romans 6:3-7; Colossians 2:12-13; Titus 3:3-7). If this is the case, how can one be regarded as obedient who denies and contradicts what the Scriptures teach? We are not speaking merely of ignorance but of opposition to the truth. Opposition to the truth cannot produce obedience.[1]

Small Steps to Apostasy

When one gets away from obedience to the Lord in small measures, it is not long before he or she takes much larger steps. A small perversion of truth today can easily lead to a large perversion tomorrow. Once obedience to the truth is abandoned, there is little to stop apostasy. I recall 20 years ago a group of Christians who believed substituting a manufactured tradition for biblical teaching was wrong. Yet they saw nothing wrong with adding instruments of music in worship because they were not substituting anything. To them adding was not as bad as substituting. They were, however, fooling themselves. If one will add to God's instructions, he or she will easily edit them with substitutions. Changing the instructions one way is as wrong as another. When obliging culture begets the practice, obedience to biblical truth soon gives way to creative exegesis. A little giving in here or there soon leads to ignoring or rewriting the text altogether. The Lord's way is forgotten; then those who call for returning to obedience are labeled as legalists.

The Bible says of Jesus, "He came to his own, and his own people did not receive him. But to all who did receive him, who believed in his name, he gave the right to become children of God, who were born, not of blood nor of the will of the flesh nor of the will of man, but of God" (John 1:11-13).

Only the Lord has a right to decide who is and is not a Christian. Popular culture can believe whatever it wishes, but it cannot overrule or edit the Lord's will. It is arrogant and presumptuous to think Jesus is subject to the whims of a new generation or that He must change His mind should He want to attract it. Jesus made it clear to Nicodemus that "unless one is born of water and the Spirit, he cannot enter the kingdom of God" (John 3:5). That teaching carried the authority of the Lord, but Jesus stated His teaching was from above (12:49-50). The early church uniformly understood that this birth of water and the Spirit referred to baptism or immersion in water (Titus 3:3-7). Yet some among churches of Christ today are debating whether an immersion is necessary or whether a sinner's prayer is sufficient to save. They are not content to follow the revealed will of God; their postmodern mindset won't let them.

God's Word Challenges Human Culture

When Paul came to Athens and Corinth, he found them filled with idols and immorality. The culture of monotheism he had known in Jerusalem was now replaced with rampant polytheism. Women were quiet in Judea but noisy and evident in Achaia. Only men were priests in Judaism, but the temple "priestesses" were plentiful in Corinth. There were nearly a thousand of them, and they acted as common prostitutes, fulfilling the carnal appetite as a means of worship. In Judea there was a book of divine law, but in Corinth all one needed to do was keep the gods appeased.

When Paul came to Corinth, he came to a foreign culture unlike the one he found in Judea, where he schooled under Gamaliel as a Pharisee. In Judea they valued righteousness; in Corinth they valued sexual immorality. The paradigm shift from a Jewish culture to a Greek one was overwhelming. The shift from modern to postmodern culture is no more radical.

We are hearing, "A new culture should require a new brand of Christianity adapted to the culture." So says the "emerging church." The church must "change or die"; so say all the postmodern experts. We have to be postmodern; we have to be pluralistic; we have to stop being judgmental about anything; and we have to stop beating up on sinners with the Bible. We need a new church for a new age!

One wonders why this insistence on reinvention did not occur when the earliest Christians moved out of a Jewish world into a Gentile one. Paul did not campaign for a reinvented church for the new Christians he converted at Corinth, Athens, Colossae or Rome. He did not argue for an accommodation to culture. He argued for the world to conform to the gospel teaching: "Do not be conformed to this world, but be transformed by the renewal of your mind, that by testing you may discern what is the will of God, what is good and acceptable and perfect" (Romans 12:2).

Paul praised those at Corinth who "maintain[ed] the traditions even as I delivered them to you" (1 Corinthians 11:2). He explained what he was preaching and how important it was for the Corinthians to stand in it and hold fast to it. He said, "Now I would remind you, brothers, of the gospel I preached to you, which you received, in which you stand, and by which you are being saved, if you hold fast to the word I preached to you – unless you believed in vain" (15:1-2). Paul did not strike a new message. He preached the one he received and expected the Corinthians to hold fast to it. He delivered the teaching he received; he did not make up something new. To take a new direction in one's faith was to believe in vain.

To the Thessalonians, Paul gave the same instruction. "So then, brothers, stand firm and hold to the traditions that you were taught by us, either by our spoken word or by our letter" (2 Thessalonians 2:15). He made no suggestion they were to follow the culture of Thessalonica and remake the church into the image of the Macedonians.

Paul carefully urged the Colossians not to be taken in by the worldly philosophies surrounding them. The Lord transferred them out of this world dominated by Satan to be the distinct, redeemed people of God (Colossians 1:13-14). He begged them to keep themselves free from the deception of the culture surrounding them.

> Therefore, as you received Christ Jesus the Lord, so walk in him, rooted and built up in him and established in the faith, just as you were taught, abounding in thanksgiving. See to it that no one takes you captive by philosophy and

empty deceit, according to human tradition, according to the elemental spirits of the world, and not according to Christ (Colossians 2:6-8).

If then you have been raised with Christ, seek the things that are above, where Christ is, seated at the right hand of God. Set your minds on things that are above, not on things that are on earth. For you have died, and your life is hidden with Christ in God. When Christ who is your life appears, then you also will appear with him in glory (Colossians 3:1-4).

Instead of accommodating culture, the Colossians were to remain established in what Paul had instructed them. Love for people did not exempt them from staying with the truth. Evangelism was not an excuse for reinventing their theology. The great evangelist Paul understood that the traditions of men would deceive them and lead them astray from the principles of Christ. Christians were to focus on Christ and on the life to come, not on the philosophies of men. Paul also understood that only the pure, undiluted gospel has the power to save (Romans 1:16). He sought eternal, timeless truth – not fickle philosophy.

The Biblical Church Is Not Worldly

Jesus said, "You are the salt of the earth, but if salt has lost its taste, how shall its saltiness be restored? It is no longer good for anything except to be thrown out and trampled under people's feet" (Matthew 5:13). The salt was to permeate the earth, not the other way around. As salt, we are to influence the people around us; otherwise we are not good for our intended purpose. When the people around us permeate us, we are not living as Christ intended. When we listen to opinion polls about what people want from a religion, we are listening to people instead of God. If we change from God's will, we will surely die because we have cut ourselves off from the source of truth and life. Our salt loses its character, and we cannot do or be what pleases God and blesses man.

When people cry for a new church, what are they thinking? They are not helping the cause of Christ. A new church? Paul said there is but one church (Ephesians 1:22-23; 4:4). A new church cannot be the one church Jesus built; it must be different. A new church is not really a church; it is a counterfeit pretending to be the real thing.

God's Word Is All That Is Needed

The living and abiding Word of God is all-sufficient. It does not lack anything needed for our salvation or for the work God has laid before us (2 Timothy 3:16-17). When the itching ears cry out for myths, the faithful gospel preacher proclaims the Word (4:1-5). He knows it will do what God purposed for it to do (Isaiah 55:8-10). He knows it truly is enough.

The disputes of our day nearly always center on biblical authority. The questions of inspiration and inerrancy have much to do with what we think the character of Scripture is. The question of all-sufficiency, however, leads to many more issues. It has been some time since our pulpits and lectureships have sounded out a cry that the Word of God is all-sufficient. So much error stems from a belief that the Word somehow does not measure up to God's desired will for our faith and practice.

Postmodernism argues that truth is so diverse that there are no absolutes or final revelations from God that cannot be dismissed or set aside for the current cultural dictates. Scripture, however, claims for itself finality and sufficiency. There is no other revealed truth from God beyond the 66 books of the Bible. Jesus promised to reveal to the apostles of the first century "all the truth" (John 16:12-13). The "faith" was "once for all delivered" ["handed down," NASB] in the first century (Jude 3). No one was to abide outside the words of Jesus. No one should transgress the Bible's finality. God takes vengeance on those who pervert His Word (Galatians 1:6-9; 2 John 9; Revelation 22:18-19).

We need nothing more than Scripture to live as God desires. Humanly designed religious beliefs and practices that go beyond the Scripture open the broad way and result in "sand" theology (Matthew 7:26-27). We need the Lord and His teaching, not the presumptuous traditions of men. We need biblical, not cultural, solutions to save us and to show us what is pleasing to God (Acts 20:32). The Word of God is final and sufficient. That is where we go to build our houses on rock. All else is sinking sand.

Questions

1. How does the lordship of Jesus Christ give direction to your life as a Christian?

2. How does the lordship of Jesus Christ give direction to the work, worship and fellowship of a congregation?

3. Why is it better to follow a course that you know is right and cannot be wrong rather than a course that might be right but could be wrong?

4. If God's Word is all sufficient, how should we respond to religious practices that are not mentioned in Scripture?

CHAPTER 3

CULTURE AND
Christianity

Culture undeniably influences each of us. Our values, language, heroes and fears unarguably arise in part from the way of life that surrounds us. Our culture, however, does not totally control us; other forces in our lives impact our thinking and behavior. If only our culture impacted our lives, we would find little room for change or growth. Man's free spirit and creativity undoubtedly keep life interesting and ever changing. Each year brings new ideas, inventions, words and understandings of life and society. Some of these new things are lies, some misperceptions, some corrupting and some destructive. We have no assurance that something is beneficial merely because it is part of our society. Culture reflects the beliefs and values of a group of people but offers no assurance these beliefs or values are necessarily from God.

In the midst of all this flux stands an unchanging, unchangeable, unrelenting, timeless, powerful and blessed message of truth, hope and righteousness. The message of Christ rises above culture because it comes from the Creator of all who is over all, through all and in all. The omniscient, all-wise God, who knows all humans better than they know themselves, has laid out for all His universal truths and precepts. These inspired eternal truths and moral laws provide a blessing by informing people of how they are to live. God has acted for our good; He has shared with us wisdom that lifts and gives hope.

Culture: The Way of the World

What is culture? In some ways, one could equate culture with what Jesus and the New Testament usually describe with the word "world." In *Christ and Culture Revisited*, D.A. Carson quoted from Richard Niebuhr's 1951 book *Christ and Culture*, which pictured Western culture this way:

> What we have in view when we deal with Christ and culture is that total process of human activity and that total result of such activity to which now the name *culture*, now the name *civilization*, is applied in common speech. Culture is the "artificial, secondary environment" which man superimposes on the natural. It comprises language, habits, ideas, beliefs, customs, social organization, inherited artifacts, technical processes, and values. This "social heritage," this "reality sui generis," which the New Testament writers frequently had in mind when they spoke of "the world," which is represented in many forms but to which Christians like other men are inevitably subject, is what we mean when we speak of culture (italics his).[1]

A culture may borrow from God, but it superimposes its own understandings upon God. It is the colored lenses by which a group of humans bring an interpreted God into focus.

Because our postmodern culture has little respect for God's timeless wisdom, it recreates its own beliefs and morals after its preferences. The postmodern mindset, rejecting the foundation of the past to empower the impulses of the present, imagines it has something better to offer than God's Word. Postmodernists loathe the judgmental and exclusive character of Christianity. They can accept the kindness and grace of Savior Jesus but will not tolerate the authoritative teaching of the Lord Jesus. They do not believe in a universal moral law controlling their lives; they would rather create their own moral rules. In their minds, the Bible is too far removed from our time and place to have any relevance or application to us today.

Postmodernists say biblical morals from another country and in another time have little to do with our morals and norms. They give lip service to God but regard His moral values as culturally obsolete and often uncouth. Having rejected absolutes of any kind, they think morality is as flexible as opinion polls. Our society loves to pick and choose its own good guys and bad guys. What God said in the beginning or in the first century does not have an influence on many people because they believe each individual is free to choose his own way. In their minds, we live in a moral democracy where we can vote on right and wrong.

Universal Truths Versus Passing Fads

Jesus, however, has not abdicated His "authority over all flesh" (John 17:2). He has neither asked our opinions nor sought our counsel in the determination of right and wrong (Romans 11:33-36). Jesus is the one true Lord, and we are not His equal. He will judge us on the last day by His eternal Word, not by our evolving standards and opinions.

My wife, Jackie, and I flew to Nashville a few months ago on a drab, cloudy day. We were weary of the cold and rain that seemed to dominate the entire trip, and we longed to see the sun and feel its warmth. As we boarded the large airliner for the trip, I remembered my first flight on an airplane many years before. I reminded myself what I had learned back then: the sun still shines above the clouds. God still rules above the clouds of culture. His sun and His eternal Word remain, even when we do not see them directly. You can mask the Lord's moral laws, you can hate Him for giving them, but you cannot make them go away. The clouds cannot remove the sun; they only block it for a time. Culture cannot remove God from His heavenly throne; it can only block Him from view for a time. God will outlast anything man can throw at Him. God is not subject to man; man is accountable to God.

The morals of Jesus will last just as long as His promises and the gospel. People want to have God's promises and love in the "good news," but you cannot have the promises of the gospel and reject its imperatives. The foundation of one is the foundation of the other. The cultural changes of our time are trying to silence the Lord, but He is still on His throne. There is but one faith, and it is for all time (Ephesians 4:5; Jude 3). In the end, the word that He spoke will still judge us. God still considers the breaking of His commandments as sin whether culture agrees or not.

The Christian morality of the New Testament is not cultural; it is universally and divinely determined and unchanging. Although we live in a framework of time, the Lord as God does not (2 Peter 3:8). What God has written in His Word stands written; it holds God's timeless authority. No one can edit it out of existence or wish it away. God still means what He says.

The Cultural Church

A longstanding debate has existed between postmodern progressives and conservatives as to whether Enlightenment thinkers such as John Locke (1632-1704) and the inductive reasoning of the rationalists brought about restoration hermeneutics or whether the hermeneutics arose from Scripture itself. But critics who wish to make New Testament Christianity the product of the Enlightenment and to make truth the product of modern rationalism actually reveal their own myopic biases. They want to impose their perception on to the truth. They are shortsighted, forgetting God's message in Christ arose in the first century. For them to allow culture to rise above Christ, they must make what is eternal into what is temporal.

In recent years, cultural churches have adopted false perceptions about what it means to love Jesus; they imagined they could love Him without listening to Him. They thought they could live in His grace but renovate His theology. Rather than view the Bible as an authoritative rule for life that they could actually read and understand, they fashioned the Bible into a symbol of confused thought, smorgasbord belief and selective morality. People cited the Bible when it supported their preconceived notions but turned a deaf ear to its commandments and precepts. They did not love so much the Jesus of the Bible as they did the Jesus they invented from selected verses. They loved a Jesus of grace but not of truth; they loved a Jesus of forgiveness but not of repentance.

Considering doctrine to be divisive, they opted for an imaginary Jesus who loved people but had no convictions about sin. Their Jesus overlooked their sins of divorce, cohabitation, homosexuality and abortion. Their Jesus marginalized His own teaching on morality and became a benign influence on culture. This mindset explains why many Christians profess faith but no longer live according to a higher standard than the "unchurched" around them.

Jesus said, "If you love me, you will keep my commandments" (John 14:15). To love Him, one must keep His commandments. What Jesus says cannot be separated from Him. He further said, "If you keep my commandments, you will abide in my love, just as I have kept my Father's commandments and abide in his love" (15:10). To think one can love the Lord and yet ignore what He teaches is an illusion. The commandments of Jesus teach us not only how to love but also how to love Him. People love God's Word because they love Him. "If anyone loves me, he will keep my word, and my Father will love him, and we will come to him and make our home with him. Whoever does not love me does not keep my words" (14:23-24). The measure of love for Jesus is whether we listen to and obey His words.

One may have strong feelings of love for God; but unless those feelings translate into obedient action, they do not demonstrate love to God.

> And by this we know that we have come to know him, if we keep his commandments. Whoever says "I know him" but does not keep his commandments is a liar, and the truth is not in him, but whoever keeps his word, in him truly the love of God is perfected. By this we may know that we are in him: whoever says he abides in him ought to walk in the same way in which he walked (1 John 2:3-6).

> By this we know love, that he laid down his life for us, and we ought to lay down our lives for the brothers. But if anyone has the world's goods and sees his brother in need, yet closes his heart against him, how does God's love abide in him? Little children, let us not love in word or talk but in deed and in truth (1 John 3:16-18).

Some in our culture speak long and loud the maxim of our need to "walk the walk" and not just "talk the talk." As postmodernists, they take it back when push comes to shove. Feelings are sufficient to them; intentions are as good as actions.

How Do Christians Live in Today's Culture?

From the beginning, two ideologies have competed for the hearts and souls of men. Satan challenged Adam and Eve's commitment to God in the garden, and sinful beliefs and practices have plagued humanity ever since. Satan has no kind intentions toward the truth. Although he masquerades as an angel of light, he remains filled with lies and wickedness (2 Corinthians 11:14-15). Jesus described the devil: "He was a murderer from the beginning, and has nothing to do with the truth, because there is no truth in him. When he lies, he speaks out of his own character, for he is a liar and the father of lies" (John 8:44).

• **Christians should distinguish worldliness from godliness.** First, because "the whole world lies in the power of the evil one" (1 John 5:19), Christians must be careful to distinguish what is sinful and worldly from what is godly and lasting. John said,

> Do not love the world or the things in the world. If anyone loves the world, the love of the Father is not in him. For all that is in the world – the desires of the flesh and the desires of the eyes and pride in possessions – is not from the Father but is from the world. And the world is passing away along with its desires, but whoever does the will of God abides forever (1 John 2:15-17).

God's ways are not man's ways (Isaiah 55:8-9), and the servant of God must take the time through the study of God's Word to know God's ways. He must know them well enough not to be "tossed to and fro by the waves and carried about by every wind of doctrine, by human cunning, by craftiness in deceitful schemes" (Ephesians 4:14). The devil is a master deceiver, and the best way to defeat him is to know the truth well enough to expose his wicked ways.

In recent years we have seen challenges to biblical teaching come in the form of new ways of interpreting the Scriptures – an existential means of understanding the Bible. Existentialism is a philosophical movement that stresses that existence is prior to essence; the concrete and individual are over the abstract and universal. Existentialism makes truth personal; what truth "means to me" is more important than what is written or the author intended. In postmodern thinking, there are no absolute truths or laws; truth becomes subjective or "what I think it is."

In today's culture that has little place for God, morality has become situational. Although Joseph Fletcher's concept of "situation ethics" has been soundly refuted as false,[2] it still dominates today's perception of morality. What is right or wrong depends on the situation one faces; right is no longer determined by biblical precept. Rather, people follow their experiences and what makes them happy. No one can be sure he is morally right because there are no moral absolutes. Consequently, there is little room for anyone to judge anyone else over any controversial behavior.

Understanding the Bible existentially and subjectively seriously challenges Bible authority. Postmodernists expect to find truth as tentative. Your truth may apply to you but not to me. One will likely hear, "You can believe that if you want to, but don't tell me what to believe." Existential thinking blends some biblical truth with cultural beliefs and in the process distorts the message of the gospel. Existential thinking ultimately leads to the belief that nothing is sinful and no one should judge anyone else for anything. Of course, this view denies God's authority is in the Word. For them the authority lies in what they think about the Word rather than what God has revealed. This belief puts God at the mercy of human culture and human judgment so that man assumes the role of authority and not God.

• **Christians should affect culture instead of being affected** *by* **culture.** Second, when the gospel confronts culture, Christians should use the gospel to change the culture to conform to God's will and not allow culture to change Christianity to conform to the will of the culture. When Paul brought the gospel to Ephesus, the penitent people who practiced magical arts came to Christ and burned their old books (Acts 19:18-20). They could see the difference between real miracles and fraudulent deception. They put an end to their whole way of life and thinking. The brethren in Thessalonica "turned to God from idols to serve the living and true God" (1 Thessalonians 1:9).

Every great reform and restoration in the Old Testament was an act of "deculturalization." With conviction and faith, prophets and kings removed the cultural ungodliness of the time. Godly people brought about the end of the culture and transformed their values and beliefs. They turned from error to the living God. Old Testament examples include:

(1) The wicked world of Noah's day called for a universal flood to wipe out the people of the earth (Genesis 6:5-8). God condemned the world and thereby saved Noah and his family. Although Noah and his family were not sinless, the overwhelmingly wicked forces were unable to influence them,

(2) Abraham left his idolatrous father and family to go to a place he did not know (Genesis 12:1-2; Hebrews 11:8-10).

(3) By the exodus, Israel came out of Egypt and left behind the gods of Egypt and the domination of Pharaoh, who was devoted to his gods. Leaving Egypt allowed the Israelites to focus on the Lord God of heaven.

(4) Elijah confronted the false prophets of Baal and Asherah on Mount Carmel. When the Lord God showed His power and presence by consuming the sacrifice with fire from heaven, the people killed the false prophets and declared "the LORD, He is God" (1 Kings 18:20-40).

(5) King Josiah removed the idolatry of his wicked grandfather Ahaz. When he heard the Law of God that Hilkiah the priest found in the temple, Josiah humbled himself and committed his heart to serve the living God. He destroyed the idols, restored the worship of the temple, and led Israel back to God (2 Chronicles 34:3-7).

(6) Ezra the priest with the prophets Haggai and Zechariah led Israel to rebuild the temple and study and obey the Law of God (Ezra 6:14-15; 7:10). So serious were the Israelites to serve God that they put away their foreign wives and children (Ezra 9, 10).

Cultural matters did not keep the faithful from doing right; when cultural matters conflicted with God's will, God's people abandoned the worldly and followed God. Compromising the essentials of the truth with the culture was never a consideration to those who would be faithful to God. Compromise takes place when two conflicting groups settle a difference by concessions on both sides – to do this is to lay the truth open to danger.

• **Christians should be transformed.** Third, faithful Christians must transform their lives to bring them into harmony with the will of God. Paul instructed us, "Do not be conformed to this world, but be transformed by the renewal of your mind, that by testing you may discern what is the will of God, what is good and acceptable and perfect" (Romans 12:2). Christians change their lives to conform to God's will by renewing their minds in a daily study of the Scriptures. When they live out their faith, they demonstrate to the world that God's way is "good and acceptable and perfect."

At this point, someone objects, "Is all of culture bad? Aren't Christians supposed to adapt to those around them?" No, culture is not all bad. Many things in various cultures have great wisdom and value; many other things are morally neutral. We are not suggesting Christians must dispose of these. We are saying faithful Christians must not conform to the worldly things that conflict with biblical truth. Paul said,

> For though I am free from all, I have made myself a servant to all, that I might win more of them. To the Jews I became as a Jew, in order to win Jews. To those under the law I became as one under the law (though not being myself under the law) that I might win those under the law. To those outside the law I became as one outside the law (not being outside the law of God but under the law of Christ) that I might win those outside the law. To the weak I became weak, that I might win the weak. I have become all things to all people, that by all means I might save some. I do it all for the sake of the gospel, that I may share with them in its blessings (1 Corinthians 9:19-23).

Wherever he went, Paul adjusted his life to share values and to reach the people he sought to teach the "unsearchable riches of Christ" (Ephesians 3:8). Although he was flexible in many things, he never forgot he was "under the law of Christ" (1 Corinthians 9:21). He did not stop living his faith although he adjusted his way of life. He did not compromise his morals although he adjusted his approach to people. He did not use this adjustment principle to overthrow plain passages of Scripture. Christians must set an example of godliness whether anyone else does. They must prove what the will of God is, what is good and acceptable and perfect. They must honor the name of Christ.

Questions

1. What are the major trends of our culture, and how are these affecting the congregation where you worship?

2. How is the golden calf fashioned by Aaron like the approach to religion promoted in the "emerging church movement"?

3. If the young adults in the church want an alternative Sunday evening service, one that is more in step with the world's style, what are the dangers it would pose to a congregation's unity and doctrinal soundness?

4. If you conducted an audit of where you have spent your time and money over the past month, what would it tell you about the influence of culture in your life?

CHAPTER 4

CULTURAL Morality

There is one thing a professor can be absolutely certain of: almost every student entering the university believes, or says he believes, that truth is relative. ... The students, of course, cannot defend their opinion. It is something with which they have been indoctrinated. – Allan Bloom[1]

If religious books are not widely circulated among the masses in this country, I do not know what is going to become of us as a nation. If the truth be not diffused, error will be; if God and His Word are not known and received, the devil and his works will gain the ascendancy; if the evangelical volume does not reach every hamlet, the pages of a corrupt and licentious literature will; if the power of the Gospel is not felt throughout the length and breadth of the land, anarchy and misrule, degradation and misery, corruption and darkness will reign without mitigation or end. – Daniel Webster, 1823[2]

Many people think it is wrong to talk about right and wrong. A Pew Forum poll in 2006 asked questions about common moral issues. Earlier polls had asked whether a behavior was moral or immoral. Remarkably, this 2006 poll added a new category in its discussion of right and wrong: "not a moral issue." Large numbers of survey respondents did not think a discussion of right and wrong should even take place on many issues. They dismissed the need to talk about whether fornication (37 percent), abortion (23 percent), excessive drinking (31 percent), or homosexuality (33 percent) were moral issues.[3] To them, sin is not an issue at all; it is not worthy of discussion.

Losing the Moral Compass

We live in a time of great moral confusion. We have politicians who say they are personally against abortion but support the mother's right to choose. It morally confuses to say, "I think it's wrong for me to take the life of an innocent unborn; but I won't oppose your taking an innocent life." When such doublespeak becomes the accepted norm, our younger generations fall into confused amorality.

Those who cannot make up their minds about right and wrong have become amoral. Amorality is an attitude or mindset in which a person is either not concerned with morals or thinks he is not open to moral judgments. In true postmodern style, the amoral have dismissed God from any authority in their lives. Amoral people finally become antinomian (against law). An "antinomian" Christian believes faith and divine grace bring about salvation and that it is therefore not necessary to submit to fixed moral laws. Antinomians believe grace is so plentiful that one need not consider sin or its consequences. They say because we are under grace and not law, we do not need to be too concerned with our transgressions. A recent Grey Matter Research & Consulting (formerly Ellison Research) report found that 13 percent of Americans do not believe at all in the concept of sin.[4]

Antinomians think by relying on grace they are magnifying it, but amorality cheapens grace. Grace becomes cheap when Christians ignore morality and repentance and take their salvation for granted. Cheap grace asserts that because grace covers all my sins, I do not need to change my moral behavior. I can continue to live as the rest of the world lives.

In contrast to cheap grace, we should remember that our salvation did not come cheap. Our salvation cost the Father His Son and cost Jesus His blood; it is costly and precious (1 Peter 1:18-19). Scripture continually reminds us of the infinite value of our salvation and the infinite debt of love we owe to God for providing it.

> For the grace of God has appeared, bringing salvation for all people, training us to renounce ungodliness and worldly passions, and to live self-controlled, upright, and godly lives in the present age, waiting for our blessed hope, the appearing of the glory of our great God and Savior Jesus Christ, who gave himself for us to redeem us from all lawlessness and to purify for himself a people for his own possession who are zealous for good works (Titus 2:11-14).

> Now this I say and testify in the Lord, that you must no longer walk as the Gentiles do, in the futility of their minds. They are darkened in their understanding, alienated from the life of God because of the ignorance that is in them, due to their hardness of heart. They have become callous and have given themselves up to sensuality, greedy to practice every kind of impurity. But that is not the way you learned Christ! – assuming that you have heard about him and were taught in him, as the truth is in Jesus, to put off your old self, which belongs to your former manner of life and is corrupt through deceitful desires, and to be renewed in the spirit of your minds, and to put on the new self, created after the likeness of God in true righteousness and holiness (Ephesians 4:17-24).

The grace of Christ does not call me to stay "just as I am." It calls me to a higher life, conformed to the image of Christ.

Cheap Grace in the Emerging Church

The emerging church has "pastors" who think they need to live as the world lives to reach the world. Thus, they are unafraid to drink alcohol with new converts, watch sexually explicit movies, or use four-letter words in front of others. They regard as heroes and "good guys" anyone who refuses to label homosexuality or abortion as sin. They speak much of the grace of Christ but lose sight that the main message of the preaching of Jesus was a call to repentance (Matthew 4:17). Chad Hall, an emergent, stated what is a common view among this group: "As one friend puts it, we need to have a 'Who Cares?' theology." [5]

Moral relativism argues there are no absolutes and no objective right and wrong. Relativists believe moral rules are merely personal preferences and arise because of one's cultural, ethnic or sexual orientation. Moral relativism has become the norm on television, in academia and among politicians. For instance, how long has it been since anyone has spoken out on television against two unmarried people sleeping with each other? How long has it been since state universities spoke out against same-sex relationships? They would not dare today.

Law and Love

In the 1960s, Joseph Fletcher argued it was sometimes right to do wrong. Philosophers such as John Warwick Montgomery and pulpits around the nation condemned his "situation ethics," but the notion of situational morality did not die. Fletcher believed love or the "agape ethic" was superior to "law ethic" so that things done out of love fulfilled God's ethic even if it violated God's law. This notion of love as a justification for our behavior has rapidly spread throughout American society.

To many people, same-sex "love" overrules God's edicts condemning homosexuality (Romans 1:24-32; 1 Corinthians 6:9-10). But love does not change sin into moral behavior. Fornication, even if two unmarried young people "love" each other, remains sinful in God's eyes. Homosexual "love" is also still sinful; it still violates God's law. Letha Scanzoni and Virginia Mollenkott argued the New Testament passages dealing with homosexuality did not include a committed, loving relationship. They said,

> The Bible clearly condemns certain kinds of homosexual practice (… gang rape, idolatry, and lustful promiscuity). However, it appears to be silent on certain other aspects of homosexuality – both the "homosexual orientation" and "a committed love-relationship" analogous to heterosexual monogamy (226).[6]

This assertion is fantasy. The Scriptures speak to all homosexual behavior whether with love or without; homosexual behavior remains condemned in Scripture.

For moral relativists, abortion is preferable to raising an unwanted child. They believe it is better to end a child's life than to have it grow up unloved or disadvantaged. Of course, they rarely consider how they may feel about that unwanted child in later days. Pro-choice people rarely speak of the long-term emotional trauma many mothers of aborted babies face.

God, however, hates taking an innocent life (Proverbs 6:16-19); and that is what abortion is. Abortion never shows love to the unborn child. It is almost as if no one considers that an unwanted child could become wanted or that adoption to a loving family is a possibility.

It never occurred to those who followed Fletcher's thinking that law defines love. They continually characterized law as a lower ethic, cold, mean-spirited, intolerant, exclusive and judgmental. They ignored the goodness and protective nature of the law.

Paul argued that "the law is good, if one uses it lawfully" (1 Timothy 1:8). God designed the law to protect the innocent from evil and ungodly sinners. God's laws are love in principle and action; they teach us how to be ethical. Moses said, "And the LORD commanded us to do all these statutes, to fear the LORD our God, for our good always, that he might preserve us alive, as we are this day" (Deuteronomy 6:24).

A wise husband knows he must learn how to love his wife. He may have the deepest of affections in his heart for her; but unless he is sensitive to what she needs, his affection will nevertheless appear insensitive and even cruel. Knowing another person's needs teaches us how to please and love that person. One loves his neighbor by fulfilling the law; "love is the fulfilling of the law" (Romans 13:8-10). The separation of an "agape ethic" from a "law ethic" is an illusion. The devil developed this two-leveled ethic myth to deceive people into thinking they can do as they please.

Christ's laws teach one how to love God and one's neighbor. Jesus said, "If anyone loves me, he will keep my word, and my Father will love him, and we will come to him and make our home with him. Whoever does not love me does not keep my words" (John 14:23-24).

The Intolerance of Inclusiveness

Moral relativists often think they are taking the higher moral ground by not judging or excluding anyone. They speak in relative terms about morality but practice judging and excluding in absolute terms. Their claim does not match their practice. Although they practice inclusiveness with the immoral person, they slander and exclude anyone who disagrees with their inclusiveness. They have become what they condemn; they merely change the criteria. They deceive themselves and blind themselves to their own hypocrisy.

Moral relativists often claim that the belief in absolute moral truth is mean-spirited, intolerant, exclusivist and judgmental. Obviously an objective view of morality will hold some things to be wrong, but the relativist contradicts himself because he also holds some things to be wrong. He believes anyone who says there is objective moral truth is wrong. This conclusion makes the relativist judgmental and possibly intolerant. If the relativist believes the absolutist to be wrong, he is just as exclusive as anyone else.

Robert Williams, a gay Episcopal priest, displayed the irreverent mindset of the moral relativist when he argued:

> The point is not really whether or not some passage in the Bible condemns homosexual acts; the point is that you cannot allow your moral and ethical decisions to be determined by the literature of a people whose culture and history are so far removed from your own. You must dare to be iconoclastic enough to say, "So what if the Bible does say it? Who cares?" [7]

Williams does not realize that he is imposing his irreverent and amoral views on those who disagree with him. He further ignores the Bible's dominating influence in America since the country's beginning and in other locations before 1776.

The Bible is unlike any other book. It shows its timeless transcendence of culture and geography. By God's design it appeals and applies to every culture in every nation in every century. Jesus sent His apostles out with the gospel to all nations for all time (Matthew 28:19-20). Jesus tasted death for all people (Hebrews 2:9). Jesus is indeed Lord of all flesh (John 17:2). The God of heaven "commands all men everywhere to repent" (Acts 17:30-31).

The moral relativists may argue moral norms arise from culture and ethnic origin, but all men find their ultimate origin in God. Differences in culture and norms do not make the Lord Jesus any less the Lord of all. Nor does their claim make the Bible any less binding upon all people in all places for all time. Jesus' words will not pass away (Matthew 24:35), and the faith was delivered once for all time to the saints (Jude 3). God's morality does not change, and no person or group of people can change it. His morality, found in His Word, is settled in heaven (Psalm 119:89). It is not going anywhere, and on the last day it will judge us (John 12:48; Revelation 20:11-15). For this reason, we must pay even more attention to what we have heard from God (Hebrews 2:1).

Interestingly, the culture that judges judgmentalism blinds its eyes to its own inconsistency. To many younger adults, judgmentalism is worse than adultery, fornication or homosexuality. They would rather stamp out judgmentalism than war, violent crimes or pollution. No one is ever supposed to say anything negative about anyone else, and anyone who does so is judgmental and mean-spirited.

According to a recent Barna organization study by David Kinnaman, 87 percent of young non-Christians believe that Christians act unchristian by being "judgmental," especially of sexual sin. Listen in on this conversation between two young adults:

> Frank says, "The Bible says homosexuality is a sin."
>
> Sally responds, "You can't say that. Who do you think you are anyway? You can't judge some person for how he was born; that's so cruel. Gay people are struggling with their self-esteem; they just want to be accepted. Jesus would never judge anybody. He loved and accepted everybody just as they were. You call yourself a Christian but you sure don't act like one. It's un-Christian to tell homosexuals they are sinners."
>
> Feeling rebuked and somewhat confused, Frank said, "But Sally, the Bible says homosexuals will not inherit the kingdom of heaven (1 Corinthians 6:9-10)."
>
> Sally responds, "Well, maybe so; but it also says not to judge. 'Judge ye not that you be not judged.' You better take the log out of your own eye before you judge somebody else."
>
> It never occurs to Sally she has judged Frank for judging.[8]

Some preachers insist "sin" is an outdated word and people should never be called "sinners." For one preacher, man's greatest need is not for forgiveness from sin but for self-esteem or self-worth. For many, to speak of sin or make people aware of their lost condition is an unchristian and uncouth strategy. Because it is insulting, it is the worst thing an evangelist can do.

People want a non-threatening Christianity, a faith with salvation and grace but without rules, judgment or the need for repentance. One preacher thundered, "We are saved by the blood not by the Book." His desire, of course, is to short-circuit preaching against sin; but if he had not heard the Book, he would not know about the blood. The same Book that tells of God's love and forgiveness also tells of God's wrath upon the impenitent.

The problem with "non-judgmentalism" is that no one can consistently practice it; it is a self-defeating belief and an impossible-to-avoid practice. If Sally condemns Frank for the act of making judgments about sin, she is herself actually just as judgmental as she thinks he is because she judged him for judging. To condemn judging is itself a moral judgment. Amazingly, she gives herself permission to react to judging by doing the very same thing.

Is Frank, however, being judgmental, or is he merely respecting the moral judgment God has given in Scripture? What if homosexuality is sinful? What if it is a learned behavior rather than a genetic trait? In May 2009 the American Psychiatric Association reversed its earlier statement made in 1998: "There is considerable recent evidence to suggest that biology, including genetic or inborn hormonal factors, play a significant role in a person's sexuality." Their new statement in a brochure called "Answers to Your Questions for a Better Understanding of Sexual Orientation & Homosexuality," says:

> There is no consensus among scientists about the exact reasons that an individual develops a heterosexual, bisexual, gay, or lesbian orientation. Although much research has examined the possible genetic, hormonal, developmental, social, and cultural influences on sexual orientation, no findings have emerged that permit scientists to conclude that

sexual orientation is determined by any particular factor or factors. Many think that nature and nurture both play complex roles.⁹

One cannot say with authority that homosexuals are born that way and not responsible for their actions.

No one thinks much of telling a friend that stealing is wrong and has consequences. What if we told all the thieves they were genetically wired to steal and not to feel bad about themselves for taking other people's belongings? Can the thief help it? What if we rebuked the victim for telling on the thief? Is the victim worse than the thief? Why should the sin of sexual immorality be different?

Being "non-judgmental" does not appeal to victims; they want justice. People tend to downplay the sins they themselves commit, but this changes when they have been sinned against. My harmless talk about you is no big deal, but your cruel gossip about me hurts deeply. I may support the sexual revolution until someone sleeps with my wife. People's attitudes change greatly when they become the "offended" rather the excuse-making "offender." Reality wakes us up. Those who demand "moral correctness" have not walked in the shoes of the offended.

One must wonder by what values and on what basis American society has learned tolerance for others. The answer lies in our Christian heritage of love for our neighbor and the example of Jesus in caring for sinners and the outcast. Many, seeing His example, think it unconscionable to reject anyone. One famous preacher even assumes that Jesus never calls anyone a sinner. But is this true?

People who know nothing else about the Bible nevertheless know Matthew 7:1, "Judge not, that you be not judged." Although they know this injunction, they do not know the setting of the passage or what else Jesus may have said about judging. For instance, Jesus said in John 7:24, "Do not judge by appearances, but judge with right judgment." Matthew 7:1 deals with the abusive judging of the Pharisees who condemned the small problems of others although they ignored their own huge problems. Jesus did not say we should never judge; He said we should watch the judgments we make and consider our own behavior.

Also, Jesus did call people sinners. In Matthew 23 Jesus scorches the hypocritical scribes and Pharisees. In Revelation Jesus rebukes various churches for tolerating doctrinal and moral sin. He demanded their repentance or threatened to remove their lampstands (their place in the kingdom of heaven). Jesus did not hesitate to tell the crowds "unless you repent, you will all likewise perish" (Luke 13:3, 5). Jesus loved sinners, but He told them to "go, and from now on sin no more" (John 8:11). Jesus did not sanctify their sins but forgave them and led them out of sin.

What some call "unchristian" arises from a myopic view of Christ. They see Him as a loving and accepting Savior but ignore the fact He will judge the world (Acts 17:30-31). Paul said, "For we must all appear before the judgment seat of Christ, so that each one may receive what is due for what he has done in the body, whether good or evil" (2 Corinthians 5:10). Jesus Himself will judge us on the basis of what is in the book (John 12:48; Revelation 20:11-15). The book and the rules do matter because Jesus is Lord just as He is Savior.

Jesus never excused sin; He never covered it up. He never lied about where sinful behavior came from to allow people to escape responsibility for it. He loved the sinner but condemned the sin and called for people to repent. He did not leave people where He found them. He hated sin so much that He was willing to die to remove the consequences of it from the people He loved.

We can fool ourselves into thinking non-judgmentalism is virtuous, but the consequences of suspending moral judgment are more and more immorality. Which is better: an immoral person with high self-esteem who fools himself into thinking his sin does not matter and who ends up lost, or a person who, realizing his sin is wrong, repents and enjoys eternal life (1 Corinthians 6:9-11)? With love, Jesus confronts sin and helps the sinner overcome it. Satan, on the other hand, tempts to sin, enjoys the sin and persecutes the brethren for exposing sin to the light.

The compassionate Christian does not enable sinners to remain enslaved to their sin by lying to them; they lift them out of that life and help them to go and sin no more.

Questions

1. How are Christians seduced into doctrinal compromise?

2. Should the church avoid discussing political issues such as abortion?

3. How is society's growing acceptance of homosexuality influencing the church?

4. How can we make clear the difference between grace and permissiveness?

CHAPTER 5

PLAYING Church

Therefore let us be grateful for receiving a kingdom that cannot be shaken, and thus let us offer to God acceptable worship, with reverence and awe, for our God is a consuming fire (Hebrews 12:28-29).

McLaren [a recognized leader in the emerging church movement] spoke at a homiletics festival in Tennessee (homiletics is the art of preaching). ... In McLaren's view, sermons about doctrine, sin, and salvation through Jesus alone create factions and should be replaced with messages about global issues. Here is how one paper covered the story. "Brian McLaren ... said many television and radio evangelists had delivered to their listeners the kind of fear-mongering and finger-pointing messages that promote factionalism. ... [He] proposed that preaching should remedy, rather than incite, controversial issues. These include poverty and climate change, and he encouraged his audience not to shy away from such global issues. 'We can't really afford to waste too many Sundays with so much at stake.'" [1]

God had a marvelous vision for what He wanted His family, the church, to be. They were to show faith devoted to His cause, be zealous for good works, stand on the truth and show love to all. They were to be compassionate to the needy, forgiving to the penitent, harmless as doves, wise as serpents, and educated in the Word. He did not want them to be children tossed to and fro by every wind of doctrine and the trickery of men. The Lord wanted them to endure healthy teaching and not collect for themselves teachers to suit their own passions. He wanted them never to turn their ears away from listening to the truth and never to turn aside to myths. He wanted them to be sober-minded, to evangelize and to fulfill their ministries. They were to deny themselves, take up their cross daily and follow in the steps of Jesus (Luke 9:23). They were simply to be obedient to everything Jesus taught.

As a church, they were the temple of God. He designed His church to be filled with washed, sanctified and justified people. They were to be holy because He is holy. They were to come out from the world and not touch what is unclean. They were not to live according to the flesh but to be transformed by renewing their minds to prove what the will of God is, what is good and acceptable and perfect (Romans 12:2). They were to be finished with the old man of sin and to conform to the image of the Son of God. They were to live lives of utter gratitude for the price Jesus paid for them.

As the church, they were the body of Christ. Their hands were to be Christ's hands. Their tongues were to be His tongue. Their heart was as His own. They were to use every gift He gave them to His glory and to build up the body. They were members of His body and recognized Him as their only head. They were to respond to His every wish. They were to be diligent workers who were not ashamed, handling the Word of God accurately (2 Timothy 2:15). They were to be noble minded, examining the Scriptures to see what was true (Acts 17:11). They were to be faithful stewards of the grace of God, the pillar and ground of the truth (1 Timothy 3:15). They were to be steadfast, immovable, always abounding in the work of the Lord (1 Corinthians 15:58).

As God's people, they represented God in the societies in which they lived. They were the salt of the earth and the light of the world. They were the essential salt needed in an otherwise bland and decaying world. They were lights in a dark world, hope to a confused world, and believers in a skeptical world. They proclaimed the excellencies of God who called them out of darkness into His marvelous light. They were the living body of Christ, the representatives for His cause, and the promoters of the gospel. They were the only Bibles some people ever read. They were the only contacts seekers for God could find.

Weak and fallible people made up the church of the first century. They often misbehaved, often misunderstood and often misplaced their priorities. The Scriptures outlined their responsibilities and their place and called them to serve and to believe. The Scriptures do the same for us. They call us to be God's people with God's heart doing God's will in God's ways. We belong to the Lord; we are not our own, for we have been bought with a price (1 Corinthians 6:20).

The Sad State of American Religion

To compare what God calls the church to be with what American religion has become must break the heart of God. American religion has become an enterprise that often forgets the God it supposedly serves. Catering to the whims of people, it has replaced worship with entertainment. Thinking success in numbers is a sign of divine approval, it has replaced evangelism with church growth. Thinking its counsel to be limited, it has replaced divine counsel with psychology. Its preachers have become pastors, academics or office managers. It has taken spiritual responsibility from parents and replaced it with activity directors. Many churches today are user-friendly, culture bound and spiritually convenient. Churches include the cross of Christ when it benefits them but not enough to turn anybody off.

When Israel strayed from the path, God sent prophets to teach them, sent disasters to humble them, and sent armies to judge them. He sent these because He cared. If He had not cared, He would have ignored them. The Lord told a disobedient Israel,

> Therefore I will judge you, O house of Israel, every one according to his ways, declares the Lord GOD. Repent and turn from all your transgressions, lest iniquity be your ruin. Cast away from you all the transgressions that you have

committed, and make yourselves a new heart and a new spirit! Why will you die, O house of Israel? For I have no pleasure in the death of anyone, declares the Lord GOD; so turn, and live (Ezekiel 18:30-32).

The opposite of love is not hate; it is indifference. God cannot be indifferent to His people when they disobey, but we cannot expect God to bless His people when they abandon His way.

Dumbing Down

Hosea said, "My people are destroyed for lack of knowledge; because you have rejected knowledge, I reject you from being a priest to me. And since you have forgotten the law of your God, I also will forget your children" (Hosea 4:6). Nothing can hurt the church of our Lord more than to silence the voice of God within. The words Jesus spoke "are spirit and are life" (John 6:63). God gave us His inspired word to teach, reprove, correct and train us. It equips us for "every good work" (2 Timothy 3:16-17). The Word builds our faith (John 20:30-31; Romans 10:17), nourishes our souls (1 Peter 2:2), strengthens our spirits (Romans 16:25), builds us up and gives us an "inheritance among all who are sanctified" (Acts 20:32). Nothing can substitute for preaching God's holy Word.

But when the Word is set aside to read the latest book by a favorite author, people starve for God. When sentimental stories substitute for the message of the cross, the people lose. When preachers preach a half gospel and neglect the whole counsel of God, the people become unbalanced. When preachers preach grace without repentance, they cheapen the power of the blood of Christ; they leave the soul incomplete and the bones broken. When preachers preach repentance without grace, they rob God of His glory and people of their hope.

Many of our preachers are afraid to preach the whole truth anymore. Instead they are preaching a dressed-down, user-friendly, nonthreatening chapel talk that contains little Scripture and little challenge. Compromised church leaders, some of whom are elders, have often made weak hirelings out of men who should be as strong as the prophets. With purse strings and authority, these ecclesiastical bullies set their hearts to silence the truth preachers ought to preach. The leaders do not want to stir up controversy, so they hush their preachers. They would rather have their flocks remain ignorant than deal with an uncomfortable conviction. By their decisions, these leaders make it clear they do not want the whole counsel of God. This silence has dumbed down the pew to the point that many in the younger generations do not know what they believe or why. The young do not even know they need to stand in the old paths of truth. Tragically, many who think they know the truth only know what they think. They know their opinions but have little biblical foundation.

Other preachers have taken it on themselves to become comedian critics of the church and the beliefs of earlier generations. They are sure the truth did not arrive until they came on the scene. With satire they poke fun at the "ignorance" of their fathers' generation. They laugh at what they consider ignorant convictions. They feel free to act without authority from Scripture and cannot understand why others object. They meet objections with caustic humor and straw-man arguments, all to the delight of the crowd; and Jesus quietly weeps.

Some preachers tell people to be immersed, but they are not clear on the reason. Some prefer immersion but will fellowship the sprinkled. Some preachers personally believe in only singing, but they will not speak against the use of instruments. They think of themselves as progressive but actually have bought into postmodernism. A postmodernist will tell you what he believes until it offends someone. Then he apologizes for his "truth" and takes it back. Of course, if he takes it back, he does not believe it. This is the true mark of a postmodernist: he will not stand for anything inconvenient. He cannot afford to offend people. It does not matter that his concession to error offends God.

Many of our adult Bible classes have become little more than fellowshiping prayer groups, long on compassion but short on Bible. Many have become an exercise in expressing opinions with little attention to God's authoritative Word. Jack Lewis described one class he visited as a "pooling of ignorance." Everyone got to say what he or she thought, except God. Other classes seem never to settle anything theological; it is as if a controversy can never be settled or must be left unsettled. There is no longer a search for what is true as long as everyone feels good when they leave class. Because we cannot offend anyone, truth must not be pressed. Let the ignorant remain ignorant; we cannot offend anyone. God is hushed once again by His own people in a Bible class. When parents do not know what they believe, they find it most difficult to educate their children spiritually. The progressives often do irreparable harm to their children by making fun of the church. How can anyone expect children to remain in the church when their parents speak disrespectfully of it? More progressive or liberal churches of Christ keep fewer than 4 in 10 (39.4 percent) of their children. Most of those who left (75.2 percent) joined some other religious group. The rest have no current religious affiliation.[2] Middle-of–the-road churches of Christ who reject extremism, on the other hand, were keeping 62 percent of their children. This is better than most religious groups in America. A recent Pew Forum article based on their U.S. Religious Landscape Survey revealed that most religions were keeping only 56 percent of their children.[3]

Yeakley also found that 12 percent of those who left after high school were actually returning to church involvement at a later time. Churches of Christ are not dying as some suppose.

Chilling Out

Popular Christianity hates religion but seeks spirituality. Many folks want to be spiritual without being religious. They do not like the forms or the formality of organized religion but love the inner graces of spirituality. They willingly forget God organized His church. Elders and deacons were God's idea (Philippians 1:1; 1 Timothy 3). Doing things "decently and in order" is still biblical (1 Corinthians 14:40). In rejecting forms and rituals, many spiritual people have also lost a sense of what is holy. They "chill" God out. By that I mean they have replaced the formal and the holy with the relaxed and the common. Their form of spirituality no longer values "reverence" for the authority and holiness of God. Instead, they prefer God to be their benign and gracious pal who does not mind how they dress, behave or worship.

Popular Christianity has done little to separate the holy from the common. Some "worship" services differ little from pop concerts. One church felt the need to offer line dancing to attract newcomers. Others advertise to "Come as you are," sending the message that church is now an informal place and needs nothing special from those who attend. Often members have forgotten they have assembled in the presence of God to worship. There is little sense of holiness. Although we sing, "Our God is an awesome God," we treat Him with little respect in our dress or attitudes. Many people dress much nicer for their jobs than they do for worship. By their actions, they proclaim their worship as a common thing, not worthy of any special effort. Yet we are a royal priesthood and a holy nation (1 Peter 2:9). The church is God's temple today (1 Corinthians 3:16; Ephesians 2:19-22).

It is common these days for Christians to come to worship late and usually dressed down. Although they can make it to their jobs and school well-groomed at 8 a.m. on other days, they can hardly come to worship by 9 a.m. For many, the day of suits with ties and Sunday dresses is over. Dressing up may be required for the job, but it is not needed for worship. It is not uncommon in the summer to see shorts, flip-flops and tank tops at church. Coming "as you are" should not be understood as "remain as I am." God expects His people to grow.

The evident attitude is that "God ought to be glad I came. Chill out! God ought to be satisfied He got anything from me at all." For many, religion has become a business enterprise. They pay their dues and get their service; nothing else should be expected from them. There is no sense of holiness in the presence of God. God deserves our best; we should not give God what is common. Worship is not an athletic event. God deserves more. He deserves to be respected in our hearts and in our appearance.

America is seeing a growing sense of release from traditional religious practices. Postmodernists are suggesting that they want more of God and less of the stuff that gets between them and their relationship with God. In fact, according to a Barna poll, 75 percent of Americans say they sense that "God is motivating people to stay connected with Him, but in different ways and through different types of experiences than in the past." Half of Americans say "a growing number of people I know are tired of the usual church experience." The results went on to say that "It is not just the survey respondents who signaled their willingness to change churches or to consider different forms of church experience. Half of all adults said they are aware of such a willingness to experiment among people they know because those individuals are tired of the common church experience." [4]

So many people think of what they want in the experience rather than think of what God expects from them in worship and service. When we assemble to worship, we are coming into the presence of God. Although our buildings are not in and of themselves sacred edifices, what we do there in worship is holy. When the Israelites gathered for worship at the temple, they did not simply show up. They lived in a world ceremonially clean and unclean. We have little sense of that. Israelite pilgrims who traveled to a feast in Jerusalem in ancient times first went to a ritual bath before they entered the temple area (John 11:55). Archaeologists count as many as 18 ritual baths surrounding the temple mount today. [5] The Scriptures symbolically link ritual purification through washing with prayer for spiritual cleansing (Psalm 51:1-2, 7-10). The purification rituals of Judaism stressed cleanliness and worthiness to serve the Lord (Leviticus 13–17; Numbers 19). Jehoiada the priest "stationed the gatekeepers at the gates of the house of the LORD so that no one should enter who was in any way unclean" (2 Chronicles 23:19).

Isaiah tells of his experience in the presence of God in the year that King Uzziah died (Isaiah 6:1-8). Seraphim proclaimed of the Lord God, "Holy, holy, holy is the LORD of hosts; the whole earth is full of his glory!" (v. 3). The Lord was sitting on His throne, lofty and exalted. The foundations of the thresholds trembled at His voice while the temple was filling with smoke. Isaiah responded, "Woe is me! For I am lost; for I am a man of unclean lips, and I dwell in the midst of a people of unclean lips; for my eyes have seen the King, the LORD of hosts!" (v. 5). Isaiah was humbled by his own sense of uncleanness before God. He expected to die because he was unclean, but God forgave him as the seraphim touched his lips with the burning coal.

When John came into the presence of the Lord Jesus on the island of Patmos, he "fell at his feet as though dead" (Revelation 1:17). He understood the awesome and special nature of the occasion.

Our worship assemblies have become so common that there is little sense of being in the presence of God or of the reverence of the occasion. The writer of Hebrews urged his readers, "Therefore let us be grateful for receiving a kingdom that cannot be shaken, and thus let us offer to God acceptable worship, with reverence and awe, for our God is a consuming fire" (Hebrews 12:28-29).

Having Fun

Churches who love the Lord and love their children rightly want to keep their children faithful in the church. The extent to which some people go to attract new converts and to hold the youth, however, reveals a remarkable shortsightedness. From their earliest days, some parents and churches have sought to train children spiritually by fun and entertaining means. We have no problem with education that is fun, but we wonder how far is too far.

Many parents think the fun some churches provide for their children can ensure their retention in the faith. However, children cannot be entertained into faith, and churches must eventually face the time when entertainment is not enough to hold them. Many young people who are involved in "youth groups" in the teen years fall away from church in their college years. Their association with the "youth group," not their faith, was the driving force in their involvement at church. When they were too old for the group, they left the faith. Fun and games alone will not keep our kids. There must be more. Fun does not cause spiritual growth.[6]

In his book *Already Gone*, Ken Ham noted the false relevancy of adapting the church to the current culture while neglecting the absolute need for teaching and training. He especially points to the use of music to capture the young.

> Even in conservative churches everyone tries to make a big deal out of praise and worship. We think that if we can make it dynamic, energetic, and fit the style of the generation we're trying to reach, the epidemic [of kids leaving the church] will be stopped and young people will start flooding back into the Church. That's simply not the case. Our research showed that music is not a fundamental factor in young adults choosing to leave or stay at a church – but the preaching of God's Word is.[7]

Ham noted that people love music, but they want good teaching. He says, "Cultural forms do not make you relevant"; they just make you cool. "Truth makes you relevant." Religious entertainment will not lead people to take up the cross of Christ or to reach spiritual maturity. I am not suggesting churches should never host activities with fellowship and fun for their children; but I am suggesting that fun without a solid, spiritual foundation will not build a saving faith that will keep them through life. If we wish to keep our children faithful, we must teach and train them.

Young people need friendship and positive influences from leaders and parents. These experiences will help them learn many basic lessons of life. They also must be nourished in the Word of God that will build their faith (John 20:30-31; Romans 10:17), strengthen them (Romans 16:25-27), and give them an inheritance (Acts 20:32). Children remain faithful through life when they are taught the Word and trained to practice what they believe. Nothing else will help them grow in faith like teaching and training (1 Peter 2:2; 2 Peter 3:18). We must grow beyond the need to have Christian basics explained to us again and again (Hebrews 5:11-14).

Does the Lord intend for the church to go to any and every length to attract new converts? Although activities that involve sports may attract athletes and open doors for the gospel, the church is not in the sports business. We are in the salvation business. Although some may find line dancing fun, one must wonder if Jesus has called us to participate in an activity often associated with nightclubs. Is this going out from the world and being "separate" (2 Corinthians 6:17-18)? How does this not violate Paul's admonition to "not be conformed to this world" (Romans 12:1-2)?

A Baptist church in St. Louis decided to use beer to attract new members. They quickly grew. Some hailed their success. The pastor said its nontraditional approach is aimed at those who are not likely to attend church. "We want to go where people are," he said. "We don't expect them to come to us." Some people think this works because the numbers have soared from 30 to 1,300, but swelling with a fleshly attraction is not the same as growth. A glass of beer will not lead one closer to the cross. It will not lead people to put to death the deeds of the flesh so they may live a new life in Christ (Colossians 3:5-11). Theological discussion in a nonthreatening environment does not sanctify inebriation and will not lead to true conversion.

Postmodern people speak of doing things "for the children" and for "church growth" to justify almost anything they want to do. References to the "children" and to "church growth" have become ready excuses for self-made religion and home-brewed churches. Because there is no biblical base for the fun they create, they excuse their worldliness on "church growth" or "the children."

When Moses went up on the mountain to receive the covenant, the Ten Commandments, the people became restless and asked Aaron to make a god for them. They ate and drank and "rose up to play" (Exodus 32:6). Moses saw the people were "out of control" and "running wild." They were worshiping a calf as the Egyptians did. Moses asked Aaron why he made the golden calf, Aaron explained:

> Let not the anger of my lord burn hot. You know the people, that they are set on evil. For they said to me, "Make us gods who shall go before us. As for this Moses, the man who brought us up out of the land of Egypt, we do not know what has become of him." So I said to them, "Let any who have gold take it off." So they gave it to me, and I threw it into the fire, and out came this calf (Exodus 32:22-24).

Frankly, some of the theological foundation for the fun at some churches makes about as much sense as Aaron's explanation. "The world does it; so to attract the worldly, we are doing it." Such foolish thinking is not evangelism; it is attraction. It does not convert one to Christ; it attracts one to the group. It does not lead people to take up the cross; it leads people to remain in their sins while thinking they are spiritual.

Questions

1. How do entertainment elements, like dramatic productions and singing groups, undermine the preaching of God's truth?

2. How are the images of God and Jesus that are used in PowerPoint presentations similar to the images introduced into Christian worship by the Catholic church of the Middle Ages?

3. Why do more liberal congregations lose a high percentage of their young people to denominationalism?

4. How do the clothes we wear to attend worship reflect our priorities?

CHAPTER 6

THE NEWLY
Defined Tolerance

The definition of new ... tolerance is that every individual's beliefs, values, lifestyle, and perception of truth claims are equal. ... There is no hierarchy of truth. Your beliefs and my beliefs are equal, and all truth is relative. – Thomas A. Helmbock[1]

Tolerance is the virtue of those who believe in nothing. Rather than stand up for what is right or wrong, the voice of tolerance says we should just let everyone be, that we'll better understand each other if we accept them as they are. – Ryan Dobson[2]

If Jesus is Lord and judge of all flesh (John 17:2), then His Word is above all. His divine truth must be superior to any man's belief. His opinion is greater and more accurate than any man's opinion. His values and morals must be higher than any ethic humans could develop. God's divine wisdom far exceeds the mind of man. If there is a God at all, then His beliefs, values, lifestyle and perception of truth are superior to any humanly devised notion. If there is a God – and there is – then all truth claims cannot be equal. What is human can

never equal what is divine. Christianity does not and cannot coexist
with the belief that all truth claims are equal.

Jesus "has a name that is above every name" (Philippians 2:9-11).
God "raised him from the dead and seated him at his right hand in the
heavenly places, far above all rule and authority and power and domin-
ion, and above every name that is named, not only in this age but also
in the one to come" (Ephesians 1:20-21). One can hardly believe in
"one Lord" (4:5) and yet be convinced every religion is equally valid
and true. One can hardly believe in one gospel (Galatians 1:6-9) and
still hold all gospels as having equal promise. Peter is right: "[T]here
is salvation in no one else, for there is no other name under heaven
given among men by which we must be saved" (Acts 4:12). To give
up our belief in the narrow path to heaven for popular culture and the
easy way is to ensure our destiny with destruction (Matthew 7:13-14).

Christians do not hold these convictions with mean-spirited hearts.
They hold them because they are true. They realize others do not or will
not hold to the truth. Some are indifferent to Christianity, and others
are offended by it. Still others are steadily growing prejudiced toward
Christianity by believing mistruths and mistaken characterizations.
Jesus told the truth when people liked it and when they did not like
it. The truth will set men free (John 8:32); but before it does, it will
surely make many angry.

The history of Christianity is speckled with confusion and persecution.
Although some would characterize Christianity as akin to Islam, one can
hardly see its history as one of oppression and the sword; instead it is a
history of bearing a cross. Although some leaders through the centuries
have abused others in the name of Christ, they cannot find a biblical
base for doing so. After all, Jesus is the Prince of Peace not a god of war.

Jesus promised, "If the world hates you, know that it has hated me
before it hated you. If you were of the world, the world would love you
as its own; but because you are not of the world, but I chose you out of
the world, therefore the world hates you" (John 15:18-19). Centuries
of persecution show that Christians have endured much for their faith.
In the 2,000 years of the Christian faith, about 70 million believers, of
whom 45.5 million or 65 percent lived in the 20th century, have been
killed for their faith.[3]

During the Sept. 12, 2006, broadcast of ABC's *The View*, Rosie O'Donnell said, "Radical Christianity is just as threatening as radical Islam in a country like America where we have a separation of church and state." [4] O'Donnell showed not only her bias against religion, especially Christianity, but also her ignorance of biblical teaching. As the Prince of Peace, Jesus urges us to be at peace with all men (Romans 12:18). This is different from the Quran 47:4 "Therefore, when ye meet the unbelievers in fight, smite at their necks; at length, when ye have thoroughly subdued them, bind a bond firmly on them: thereafter is the time for either generosity or ransom, until the war lays down its burdens. ... But those who are slain in the Way of Allah, He will never let their deeds be lost." The New Testament never teaches Christians to kill or to enslave unbelievers they cannot convert.

The word "love" can be found fewer than 70 times in the Quran (22 of which refer to whom Allah does *not* love), whereas forms of the word "love" appear more than 400 times in the King James Version of the Bible. The Bible makes it clear that love is first in importance (Deuteronomy 6:4; Matthew 22:37-40; 1 Corinthians 13:1-3). Love conquers evil and fear. God Himself is love; and "[w]e love because he first loved us" (1 John 4:8, 19). God commands us to love one another and even our enemies. Such ideas are not found in the Quran. Christianity is nothing like Islam. Although Muslims claim Allah is the God of the Bible, he is no more Jehovah than one of Jeroboam's golden calves.

Freedom of Speech

In 1954 the Johnson Amendment came into law at the urging of U.S. Sen. Lyndon B. Johnson who was facing stiff opposition to his reelection from nonprofit Christian groups. Preachers in Texas were speaking their minds from the pulpit. The Johnson Amendment inserted language into the Internal Revenue Service code that banned nonprofit organizations and churches from supporting or opposing candidates for political office. According to Brad O'Leary, "The 'Johnson Amendment,' now codified as part of 26 U.S.C. sec 501(c)(3), states that a tax-exempt organization may not 'participate in, or intervene in (including the publishing or distributing of statements), any political campaign on behalf of (or in opposition to) any candidate for public office.'" [5]

This action "should have been seen as a clear infringement of the First Amendment back in 1954 but it wasn't," writes Joseph Farah. "And this most regrettable action has haunted America ever since." [6]

As time has passed, the U.S. government has continued to infringe on religious freedom with the outlawing of prayer and Bible reading in the schools and ignoring the First Amendment. Many Americans today have little understanding of the high regard the founders of the Constitution had for Christianity and for the Bible. The First Amendment ratified in 1791 simply says: "Congress shall make no law respecting an establishment of religion, or prohibiting the free exercise thereof; or abridging the freedom of speech, or of the press; or the right of the people peaceably to assemble, and to petition the Government for a redress of grievances." The Johnson Amendment and more recent hate-crimes legislation forbidding preachers from proclaiming biblical teaching on current issues clearly violate the First Amendment.

In 2009, Congress and the president pushed for a bill against hate crimes including criminalizing speaking out against another's sexual orientation. The belief is that by preaching it is a sin to be homosexual one may incite violence against homosexuals and be guilty of a hate crime. This bill creates an enormous dilemma for many churches who seek to preach the whole counsel of God and yet do not wish to be labeled as those who hate. The number one criticism most outsiders age 16-29 have against Christians is they are "unchristian" toward homosexuals by saying their behavior is sin.[7] More than 9 in 10 (91 percent) said Christians were anti-homosexual. Because of this, they regard Christians as judgmental (87 percent) and hypocritical (85 percent) – saying one thing (love everyone and don't judge) while doing another (hypocritically judging and hating homosexuals). Incredibly, these late adolescents and young adults see no problem with judging Christians for judging sin. In the minds of young postmodernists, the judgmental behavior of Christians (speaking against sin) entitles postmodernists to be judgmental and intolerant toward Christians.

When *In Search of the Lord's Way*, the TV program on which I speak, mentions the word "homosexual," we can be sure one or two broadcast stations will not air the program. We wish the station managers would air the program, but they have to live with their decisions to air some past program. On some other stations, the station managers are afraid to air any program speaking negatively about homosexuals. Their objection is not based on either support for homosexuality or an opposition to Christianity. They will not air the program because they fear homosexual groups will burn down the TV station! These groups believe rejection somehow permits them to be violent. When some misguided Christian kills an abortionist, other Christians condemn the action. But when Christians speak out against sin, people think their "intolerance" allows an aggressive response. Who are the mean-spirited? Are they the ones who speak God's Word in love, or are they the ones who hate so much to hear the truth they are willing to burn down a TV station?

Preaching the truth of God's Word, including repentance, is not hateful. It is the path to correction. When you hear the word "repentance," I hope you do not think of something negative. Repentance is a precious opportunity to make a new life that is pleasing to God. The Bible describes repentance as a gift:

> The God of our fathers raised Jesus, whom you killed by hanging him on a tree. God exalted him at his right hand as Leader and Savior, to give repentance to Israel and forgiveness of sins. And we are witnesses to these things, and so is the Holy Spirit, whom God has given to those who obey him (Acts 5:30-32).

Peter and the Jews rejoiced in Acts 11:18 that God had granted repentance to the Gentiles. And we should rejoice too! The opportunity to repent, to change our hearts and lives, is a great gift. We do not have to be stuck in a life of sin separated from God. We can come to Him and enjoy His love and grace forever.

Imagine that you are driving down the highway and come upon an automobile accident. When you pull over to the side of the road, you find an injured woman with a broken leg. She is in great agony and crying out for help. You immediately call 9-1-1, and an emergency medical team is dispatched. The technician gets to the scene and hears the woman with the broken leg crying out, "Give me something to deaden the pain! Give me something to deaden the pain! Just knock me out!" Surely the technician will give her something to ease the pain; but he will not stop there. He will set the leg so that it can heal. If the leg is not set back into place, it will be warped. The problem must be corrected if the woman is to be whole and healthy. It may hurt terribly to set that leg, but it would be far worse to leave it broken. We go to the doctor to find healing.

The Word of God will heal those who embrace it wholeheartedly and completely. Good spiritual health requires many things. One cannot pick and choose which instructions of God are okay and which will be thrown out. Tolerance is not a license to edit God's truth, God's morals or God's teaching. Obedience means to do what is right regardless of the cost, not simply to comply with what we like. Selective obedience is not really obedience at all. It does not trust God to speak what is right on every occasion. It pushes human wisdom to dictate to God. It insults God by making Him common and makes man the measure of all things.

Some beliefs are false, and we instinctively know them to be false. Calling them true does not make them equally valid with Christianity. Tolerance does not turn a lie into a truth or immorality into ethical behavior. God's definition of right and wrong stands written. Counting all those in favor of a fallacious, human notion does not change what God says about the matter. "Let God be true though every one were a liar" (Romans 3:4).

The philosophical basis for this new tolerance is a combination of secularism, pluralism and privatization. Ravi Zacharias correctly observed:

> Secularization led us to a loss of shame, pluralization to a loss of reason, and privatization to a loss of meaning. We noted that when secularization has bred its loss of shame it will generate evil even against those we love. Pluralization in turn has given birth to the loss of reason, generating evil toward those whom we choose to hate. Privatization kills meaning and gives rise to evil against ourselves because the alienation within mutilates the soul.[8]

Religious Pluralism Is Self-Contradictory

When I hear people embrace the need for tolerance because of religious pluralism, I wonder if they should not ask themselves what this argument says about the objective truth claims of Christianity. One cannot at the same time argue for the risen Jesus Christ as the "one Lord" while embracing a tolerant religious pluralism that makes Jesus merely one religious voice among many choices. It goes against reason to think Jesus is the only Lord of all flesh while putting Buddha and Muhammad on the same level. Religious pluralism will not allow comparison, will not allow critical thinking, and will not allow convictions based on reason. Pluralism makes its adherents agnostics; they cannot commit to anything with finality. Religious faith becomes uncritical preference.

Religious pluralism denies the right of its adherents to rise above subjective choices. They can never recognize the fundamentals of Christianity as objective truth. To claim that religious truth is relative and subjective, they must label biblical Christianity as false. For them, New Testament Christianity is not true for all; it is merely the preferred belief of some. They will not admit the binding nature of Christianity on anyone. Religious pluralism, in committing itself to the view that all religions are equally true, condemns those religions that take the opposite view as false. If Christianity is uniquely true, then according to religious pluralism it must be false. Religious pluralism is therefore self-contradictory. If religious pluralism is true, then every religion is true. If each religion is true, then it must be relatively true and never authoritatively true. There can be no really true religion in a culture of religious pluralism. True religion for them is a fantasy. Such irrational and contradictory statements leave us staggering in confusion.

When religious pluralists contend everyone ought to be a pluralist, the tolerance argument for religious pluralism becomes, by its own standards, intolerant. If tolerance is of overriding importance, then religious pluralists should also tolerate Christians. Why should Christians be excluded from having objective and absolute convictions? Why are Christians not allowed to hold their so-called "intolerant" beliefs? The so-called "tolerant" are not tolerant if they will not tolerate those with whom they disagree over the uniqueness of Christ. In truth, they tolerate only people who agree with their agnostic approach to religion.

Religious pluralism is deceptively self-contradictory, and the argument for tolerance is, by its own standard, intolerant. When critical thinking and comparative studies are neutered by a whimsical and imaginary tolerance, people lose the freedom to disagree. Religious pluralism claims to embrace the virtue of tolerance, but it only changes the boundaries of intolerance. It moves the boundaries from objective, critical thinking to subjective opinions. We cannot break religious intolerance by pretending to suspend judgment. We break it by holding fast to everlasting truths while treating others with patience, gentleness and respect.

True Christians can say what must be said about error when they say it in love. They do not have to apologize for speaking the truth, nor should they take the truth back. Some Christians, to be sure, have abused others with the truth; but this does not make the truth less true. Abusive behavior is no credit to Christianity, but the abuse of a thing does not argue against its valid use. Those who rightly call attention to the abuses of the Inquisition or of the Crusades must look to sources other than Christ although the abusers claimed the participants were acting in God's name. Jesus never sanctioned torture or war; Christianity has no jihad. Its war is against sinful ideas, not nations. Christianity's power arises not from the sword but from its ability to pierce and change the heart and soul. It does not make converts with a sword but with its message of faith, hope and love. Jesus said, "And I, when I am lifted up from the earth, will draw all people to myself" (John 12:32). The message of the cross reaches deep into the innermost being of any man or woman who takes the time to hear it. Christians are in the saving business, the lifting business. Jesus "gave himself for our sins to deliver us from the present evil age, according to the will of our God and Father" (Galatians 1:4).

> And the Lord's servant must not be quarrelsome but kind to everyone, able to teach, patiently enduring evil, correcting his opponents with gentleness. God may perhaps grant them repentance leading to a knowledge of the truth, and

they may … escape from the snare of the devil, after being captured by him to do his will (2 Timothy 2:24-26).

Christians want everyone to be saved, but salvation without correction is a fantasy. "Just as I Am" does not mean "this is how I'm going to stay." God expects people to make changes in their lives.

Those who think it unchristian for the church to be intolerant toward sin have missed the point about Jesus. His main message was repentance (Matthew 4:17). He loved and took time with sinners, but His message was "[G]o and … sin no more" (John 5:14; 8:11). The church could not tolerate sin in its midst because "a little leaven leavens the whole lump" (1 Corinthians 5:6; Galatians 5:9). Doctrinal or moral error on the part of one can infect the whole church. Paul rebuked the church at Corinth for its attitude toward a man in great sin: "It is actually reported that there is sexual immorality among you, and of a kind that is not tolerated even among pagans, for a man has his father's wife. And you are arrogant! Ought you not rather to mourn? Let him who has done this be removed from among you" (1 Corinthians 5:1-2). Removing the source of infection was necessary to the health of the congregation.

In Revelation 2, Jesus spoke to a problem of tolerating sin. Although the church at Ephesus had other problems, Jesus praised them because they "cannot bear with those who are evil" (Revelation 2:2). The church at Ephesus tested those who came to them and found men to be false. The church at Thyatira, however, began tolerating sin. Jesus will not forever put up with churches that tolerate doctrinal or moral error. Jesus is not morally neutral; He hates sin and calls on us to despise it as well (Romans 12:9). We must understand there is an end to the patience of God. God will not tolerate His children if they tolerate sin unchecked. Jesus spoke directly and forcefully to the church at Thyatira:

> But I have this against you, that you tolerate that woman
> Jezebel, who calls herself a prophetess and is teaching and
> seducing my servants to practice sexual immorality and to
> eat food sacrificed to idols. I gave her time to repent, but
> she refuses to repent of her sexual immorality. Behold,
> I will throw her onto a sickbed, and those who commit

adultery with her I will throw into great tribulation, unless they repent of her works, and I will strike her children dead. And all the churches will know that I am he who searches mind and heart, and I will give to each of you according to your works (Revelation 2:20-23).

The Lord will step in and act against a church if that church fails to do so. The church belongs to the Lord, and He will not let sin destroy it. We may easily deceive ourselves by thinking the Lord is too good and gracious to act harshly against sin, but the Lord takes sin seriously. He simply will not put up with continued disobedience; "[i]t is a fearful thing to fall into the hands of the living God" (Hebrews 10:31).

Sin deceives, blinds, hardens, enslaves and ultimately kills those who practice it. Those who are caught up in error will inevitably criticize and strike out at those who possess the same frailty. People tend to judge others harshly for the things they most despise in themselves. Amazingly, they make these judgments in blindness, oblivious to their hypocrisy. It is easier to condemn common faults in others than it is to repent of our own sins.

"Correct" Pharisees come in all kinds because people tend to pretend. A hypocrite pretends to be what he never intends to be; he is an actor. Just as the Pharisees deceived themselves that they were above others, so the "correct" crowd believes its ethics are superior to those of the Christian. Jesus exposed the Pharisees to be self-righteous sinners who as the "elite" of their day viewed others with contempt (Luke 18:9). The "politically correct" and "religiously correct" crowd with a postmodern mindset also views with contempt anyone who does not agree. Many in today's culture embrace self-righteous judgmentalism, not tolerance; they merely rename it "correctness."

They remarkably strain out a gnat and swallow a camel (Matthew 23:24). The Pharisees set aside the Law of God to maintain their human traditions (15:1-14). They hated Jesus for speaking out against their pretentious ways. Jesus did not die because He was evil; He died because He exposed the evil of the time. Today the "correct" crowd harshly condemns the person who speaks against sin although he does no wrong. At the same time, they make a hero of one who practices an abomination. The preacher is condemned as unchristian and mean-spirited for speaking out against homosexual sin while society and the law give the homosexual special status and protection. Freedom to speak religious truth falls to the special lusts of perverted souls (Romans 1:24-32).

We return to the place we started with this chapter. Because Jesus is Lord and judge of all flesh, the many conversations about "correctness" are meaningless. Jesus' Word is final. Even if only faithful Christians regard His Word as final, nothing is changed. The Word stands written! No human or group of humans can dismiss, delete or edit it. It stands because it is God's holy Word. It will stand when heaven and earth are gone (Matthew 24:35). Christians ultimately must decide whether they will hold to God's eternal truth or the passing notions of the generation. When the people of God said "no" to God and rebelled against Him by embracing the popular beliefs of the nations around them, they soon found the wrath of God. We should learn from that and hold fast to the things God has revealed. Adrian Rogers has correctly said:

> It is better to be divided by truth than to be united in error. It is better to speak the truth that hurts and then heals, than falsehood that comforts and then kills. … [I]t is not love and it is not friendship if we fail to declare the whole counsel of God. It is better to be hated for telling the truth than to be loved for telling a lie.[9]

Questions

1. How has political liberalism hindered the open teaching of God's truth?

2. Why does our society try to make Islam acceptable? What are the consequences of this attempt?

3. In what ways is religious pluralism self-contradictory?

4. Why is the doctrine of repentance at odds with a pluralistic approach?

CHAPTER 7

BULLIED BY
Perceptions

I know you think you know what I'm saying, but what you think I'm saying and what I am actually saying may not be the same thing. – Unknown

All propaganda has to be popular and has to adapt its spiritual level to the perception of the least intelligent of those towards whom it intends to direct itself. – Adolf Hitler, *Mein Kampf (My Struggle),* Vol. I

P erceptions shape our thinking and our lives. Some spiritual perceptions, like the physical ones, accurately reflect what is happening. Others only seem true. If we look closely at an optical illusion, we will see first what is most obvious. With a little more inspection, we might see something different. One thing is real; the other is illusory.

No doubt you have seen the famous optical illusion in the shape of a goblet. On closer examination it appears to be two identical profiles of people facing each other. Reality says it is a goblet; the illusion says it is two people. The contrived appearance can mask the true object.

Spiritual Deception

When people do not like the truth, they set the stage for an alternative to take its place. Willfully ignoring some things and recasting others, they position a lie to appear as the truth. The prophet Isaiah saw this behavior in his day. "Woe to those who call evil good and good evil, who put darkness for light and light for darkness, who put bitter for sweet and sweet for bitter! Woe to those who are wise in their own eyes, and shrewd in their own sight" (Isaiah 5:20-21). Those who contrive perceptions think they have done something amazing. They think they are wise and shrewd, pulling the wool over everyone's eyes; however, one cannot hide the truth forever. It will surface and expose the "ravenous wolves" in "sheep's clothing" (Matthew 7:15).

Satan "disguises himself as an angel of light. So it is no surprise if his servants, also, disguise themselves as servants of righteousness. Their end will correspond to their deeds" (2 Corinthians 11:14-15). It is common for those sold on sin to deceive others by turning things upside down. They think they can fool others by casting the light on an illusion. Some do buy into their illusory beliefs, but they do not fool God. They will not fool faithful Christians because God provides the truth in His Word. The weak and ignorant, however, fall prey to misguided schemes.

Following the Broad Way

Advertisers love to tell us that a product is the "fastest growing" or "largest selling" because they do not have to convince us directly the product is good; they need only say that many others think so. In their minds, this is proof enough. When charity telethons spend much time listing everyone who contributes to their cause, they communicate the message to the holdouts: "Look at all the people who have decided to give. It must be the correct thing to do." Television producers know they can make a weak joke funnier with canned laughter. This is the principle of "social proof": people use other people to see if what they believe is true. The tendency to see an action as more suitable when others are doing it works well. This is why many people travel 75 miles an hour on inner-city freeways where the speed limit is 60. People believe and do things they would not usually do because the people around them are doing it. Cavett Robert, a sales motivation consultant said, "Since 95 percent of the people are imitators and only 5 percent initiators, people are persuaded more by the actions of others than by any proof we can offer." Blindly following the crowd sounds much like the Lord's description of the wide gate and the easy way (Matthew 7:13-14).

When people are uncertain what to do, they are more likely to use others' actions to decide how they themselves should act. But social proof works most powerfully when we are seeing people who are just like us. The more similar people are to us, the more likely they are to influence our behavior. People often think of teenagers as rebellious or independent. This is typically true when teens interact with their parents, but when teens conform and comply with their peers, they do what social proof tells them is proper.

People can hear a half-truth or a mostly true statement again and again until they believe it to be entirely true. Joseph Goebbels, Adolf Hitler's propaganda minister, said, "If you tell a lie big enough and keep repeating it, people will eventually come to believe it." [2] But even if people do temporarily believe it, the contrived perception will not last forever. Goebbels knew the state must keep the people from finding out the whole truth. The quote continues: "The lie can be maintained only for such time as the State can shield the people from the political, economic and/or military consequences of the lie. It thus becomes vitally important for the State to use all of its powers to repress dissent, for the truth is the mortal enemy of the lie, and thus by extension, the truth is the greatest enemy of the State." Satan may blind the weak, the ignorant and the gullible who will not search out the truth, but the truth will not disappear. Propaganda has the power to deceive only until the truth surfaces.

The Scriptures say of the Bereans, "Now these Jews were more noble than those in Thessalonica; they received the word with all eagerness, examining the Scriptures daily to see if these things were so" (Acts 17:11). Christians have a duty to test what they hear and measure it by God's Word. The Scriptures are God's standard of moral and religious truth, and Christians who ignore that standard soon find themselves compromised. How badly we need the Berean spirit that eagerly searches out what God wills and sets aside everything else! We do not need human experts in sociology to decide the behavior of our churches; we need the Bible. We do not need marketing polls to decide how we should look; we need to mirror the faithfulness of the Lord. God will take care of His people.

Appearing religious does not equal being righteous. The Pharisees took great pains to appear godly and religious, but their self-righteousness did not impress God. Jesus gave His harshest reproof to the hypocrisy of the scribes and Pharisees, pronouncing repeated woes on them as "whitewashed tombs" full of dead men's bones (Matthew 23:13-33). Appearance is not everything because appearances do not last. One may be able to fool others for a time, but God will one day reveal hidden secrets (Romans 2:16; 1 Corinthians 4:5).

Our wish is for the salvation of all, even those who are deceived by their own self-righteousness. Paul said this about the Jews:

> Brothers, my heart's desire and prayer to God for them is that they may be saved. For I bear them witness that they have a zeal for God, but not according to knowledge. For, being ignorant of the righteousness of God, and seeking to establish their own, they did not submit to God's righteousness. For Christ is the end of the law for righteousness to everyone who believes (Romans 10:1-4).

Their righteousness, because it did not conform to God's truth, proved illusory; and a heart full of zeal did not change this. Those who suggest that the zealous heart trumps mistaken beliefs cannot explain why the Jews are not saved. Zeal does not turn a lie into the truth. A deceived zealot is still deceived. To encourage such a zealot in his deception is cruel. Paul wanted them to know the truth rather than to remain ignorant.

Some Propaganda Principles and Techniques

With propaganda and bullying, one can temporarily create an environment lacking truth. Goebbels believed propaganda made the Third Reich. Germany fell prey to Hitler's propaganda machine because Hitler effectively employed principles and techniques designed to shut out any opposition. He took complete control over the news and entertainment media and soon regimented all German culture. Goebbels used his skills as an orator to exploit the emotions of the mobs, stirring and intimidating people to do things they would never have done otherwise. The Nazis systematically killed an estimated 6 million Jews and were responsible for an estimated 11 million additional deaths during World War II. Hitler deceived his own people, but he could not deceive the Allies forever.

Hitler found success in Germany by using propaganda that got the people's interest. His minister, Goebbels, violently suppressed any material that could provide the enemy with useful information to offset his agenda. The Hitler machine spoke in tones that led their enemies to draw the conclusions the Nazis wanted. Hiding the truth about Hitler, Goebbels goaded his enemies to reveal information about themselves. Hitler and Goebbels made reference to an enemy's propaganda only when it helped decrease the enemy's prestige or lent support to their own objective. They carefully and craftily timed their propaganda and began it at the ideal moment. They wanted to speak before their opponents had opportunity. The Nazis pre-labeled people and events with distinctive phrases and slogans to evoke the desired response and then repeatedly used these slogans and labels.

One of Goebbels' staff members, Elizabeth Noelle-Neumann, later explained how the Nazis silenced their opponents with a theory she named the "spiral of silence." She wondered why the Germans supported wrong political positions that led to national defeat, humiliation and ruin in the 1930s and 1940s. The spiral of silence occurs when those individuals who perceive their opinion is popular express it; whereas those who do not think their opinion is popular remain quiet. This occurs in a spiral so that one side of an issue ends with much publicity and the other side with little. The silence of the opposition grows out of the fear of isolation. It is not just a matter of wanting to be on the winning side, but it is an attempt to avoid being isolated from one's social group. Threats of criticism from others were found to be powerful forces in silencing individuals.[3]

Hitler and his leadership focused on indoctrinating the youth with their beliefs. They would tolerate no other political view. They wanted unobstructed loyalty to the Nazi cause. They were raising an armed generation in their image. Hitler said in 1938:

These boys and girls enter our organizations [at] ten years
of age, and often for the first time get a little fresh air; after
four years of the Young Folk they go on to the Hitler Youth,
where we have them for another four years ... And even if
they are still not complete National Socialists, they go to
Labor Service and are smoothed out there for another six,
seven months ... And whatever class consciousness or social
status might still be left ... the Wehrmacht [German armed
forces] will take care of that.[4]

Hitler knew peer pressure among youth was strong, and their minds
were not mature enough for critical thinking against his agenda. He
believed he could overcome whatever parental training these young
Germans received. He wanted Nazis.

Churches too sometimes find themselves with leaders whose agenda
differs from Scripture. Peter warned:

[T]here will be false teachers among you, who will se-
cretly bring in destructive heresies, even denying the Master
who bought them, bringing upon themselves swift destruction. And many will follow their sensuality, and because
of them the way of truth will be blasphemed. And in their
greed they will exploit you with false words. Their con-
demnation from long ago is not idle, and their destruction
is not asleep (2 Peter 2:1-3).

People tend to hide the unpleasant truths from themselves, repress-
ing what they believe to fit into the social situation. Parents of teens
whose youth minister is leading the youth in the wrong direction will
often remain silent because their child is at least involved in church.
People whose church is rapidly changing for the worse often sit back
and do nothing; some are more attached to a building or to a school
than to the Lord. They fear rejection if they dissent from the perceived
popular view. Of course, counting noses does not decide truth. The
10 spies who brought back the bad report won the popular opinion,
but at what cost? The largest congregation in the world is not the
Lord's church if the Lord does not rule it.

The progressive movement in churches of Christ is making its temporary inroads by pressing perceptions. Its supporters argue that because many people are beginning to make changes everyone else should too. They paint themselves as the caring and godly leaders of the future and pre-label the traditionalists as mean-spirited legalists and Pharisees. They dig in the archives to find old and failed arguments to hoodwink the new generation. They tell the church that unless everyone follows their advice, the church will surely die. They label casual as good and formal as old. They replace evangelism with conversations and good deeds. They say sin, repentance and hell are outdated messages and rewrite the doctrine of grace. They decide to remain silent on the self-made religion of the musical instrument, figuring their silence would end the opposition; and they privately whisper to the weak and naive that "*psallo* in the New Testament means we can play instruments." With great deceit they lead the unsuspecting astray.

To the progressives, disagreeing with them means you are ignorant and legalistic. Disagreeing means you are going against the academic beliefs of many of our Christian schools, showing your lack of scholarship. If you disagree, you are not one of the elite. You are holding the church back from being like its religious neighbors. You want the church to die. You do not care about people. You do not understand grace. You are blind. The progressive group that claims to love people pulls out its fangs against brethren who disagree. They will not tolerate dissent but consider anyone who disagrees as backward and ignorant.

Progressives tell older Christians who cannot adjust to the changes that their place at church is not as important as winning the outsiders. They regard them as unfaithful troublemakers who should be pushed aside to achieve their agenda. To some progressives, objectors are collateral damage. Progressives who take power over a congregation give these unyielding brethren little alternative but to leave should they dissent.

Me Versus My Parents

Postmodernists revolt at anything "modern." (By the strange twist of language, "modern" no longer means "up-to-date," but rather it now means "old fashioned.") They do not like the traditional, what they usually define as what their parents or grandparents believed and practiced. They especially do not like "church" as their parents practiced it, so they try to remake church according to their own preferences. They will dress casual instead of wearing the formal suit and dress. They will sing the new songs and ignore the old ones. They will trade off the sermon for conversations, dramas, interviews and special events. They no longer need an invitation at the conclusion of a sermon. They desire to gather in groups for devotionals rather than assemble as a whole body. Sunday night worship is optional if there is some other group action taking place. It does not occur to them that the constant drain from assembling says to young folks that assembling isn't important.

If their parents did it, many postmodern children do not want it. After all, their parents do not know the Lord the way their postmodern friends do. The old, traditional preacher back home does not think about the Bible the way their friends do. All parents want to do is to keep the church the way it was in the 1950s. The "modern" generation with its authoritative approach and logic had it all wrong. They were exclusivists, arrogant, judgmental and mean-spirited. They thought they were the only ones going to heaven. In their hearts, the postmodernists believe, "Now we know better. We know God's grace reaches everyone who loves Him, even if they are mistaken in their understanding about baptism."

Some postmodernists delight in slapping down their parents and their parents' religious beliefs. They seem bound to accept as moral whatever practice their parents condemned and consider valid whatever belief their parents criticized. They think they are more "authentic" than their parents, whom they picture as caught up in appearances. They use the word "authentic" (an example that measures up without pretense) in odd ways. They use "authentic" to mean no pretense. They are not hypocrites but try to be real. That is commendable because no one likes a phony.

What is not commendable is that they confuse "authentic" with not trying to live the godly life. Authentic to them means "this is the way I am, and I don't need to change. Accept me as I am, and I don't have to do better. I don't have to correct my misunderstandings or my un-christian behavior. I am authentic to my ways." Instead of controlling their tongues, they think using four-letter words is more "authentic." Instead of remaining free from alcohol, they think drinking a beer with a friend is more "authentic" as a Christian. Instead of keeping their minds pure, some think going to a sexually explicit movie is more "authentic" as a Christian. I am not speaking merely of people in the pew here; I am speaking of some church leaders who call sinful activities "authentic Christianity."

Judgmental Versus Inclusive

To postmodernists, inclusiveness always trumps judgmentalism. A clear example of this approach is seen in President Barack Obama's attitude towards homosexuality, described in this story from The Associated Press:

> At a White House celebration of Gay Pride Month, Obama said he hopes to persuade all Americans to accept homosexuality. "There are good and decent people in this country who don't yet fully embrace their gay brothers and sisters – not yet," said the president. "That's why I've spoken about these issues – not just in front of you – but in front of unlikely audiences, in front of African-American church members."
>
> Obama acknowledged that many Americans still disapprove of homosexuality. "There are still fellow citizens, perhaps neighbors or even family members and loved ones, who still hold fast to worn arguments and old attitudes," he stated.[5]

President Obama believed that those who grudgingly embraced the old "worn" arguments from biblical times could nonetheless (and surprisingly) still be "good and decent people," despite their objection to homosexuality. The article ended by stating, "The audience at the White House ceremony included Episcopal Bishop Gene Robinson and other homosexual clergy. Obama introduced Robinson as a 'special friend.' " Robinson divorced his wife of 15 years and is now involved in a homosexual relationship. Are these values somehow higher than the value of faithfulness to a marital vow? The perception is that being true to ourselves is more important than keeping commitments to our family and that being nonjudgmental about others is a higher ethic than God's morality.

The distinction here is between morality and no morality. When one buys into the deceptive perception that inclusiveness and nonjudgmentalism are the umbrella ethic that covers sin and immorality, then one has bought into amorality, the suspension of morality. The only taboo of nonjudgmentalism is to recognize any moral sin. Nonjudgmentalism obligates us to turn a blind eye toward sin. We must pretend it is not sin and is not harmful. All are then free to practice any behavior they want. Despite it all, the inclusivist bullies anyone who breaks his moral law of inclusivism. The popularity of nonjudgmental inclusivism has taken hold on a generation of Americans. Just let anyone make a moral distinction, and this inclusivist generation feels empowered to criticize and censure. This is how the spiral of silence has captured the minds of our young adults to embrace the freedom of homosexuality and call Christians who disagree "unchristian," "hypocrites" and "mean-spirited." Paul warned the Colossians:

> Therefore, as you received Christ Jesus the Lord, so walk in him, rooted and built up in him and established in the faith, just as you were taught, abounding in thanksgiving. See to it that no one takes you captive by philosophy and empty deceit, according to human tradition, according to the elemental spirits of the world, and not according to Christ (Colossians 2:6-8).

Questions

1. How are teenagers and young adults at a high risk of being manipulated by false teachers?

2. If the teenagers or young adults of a congregation begin meeting in a separate worship service on Sunday evenings, one designed to be more "contemporary," what are the dangers this approach poses?

3. Why are teenagers and young adults in danger of being drawn into a personality cult of a magnetic leader?

4. What dangers of manipulation exist in small groups, retreats and other special settings?

CHAPTER 8

THE VANISHING
of Heresy

The net result of all these impulses to pluralism is that ...
there are just about as many theologies as there are theolo-
gians to devise them; the concept of heresy has almost lost
its meaning; and loyalty to the institutional church has for
the most part taken the place of loyalty to the faith once for
all delivered to the saints, for no one is quite sure any more
what the essence of that faith really is. – J.I. Packer, 1987 [1]

I appeal to you, brothers, to watch out for those who cause
divisions and create obstacles contrary to the doctrine that
you have been taught; avoid them. For such persons do not
serve our Lord Christ, but their own appetites, and by smooth
talk and flattery they deceive the hearts of the naive. For
your obedience is known to all, so that I rejoice over you,
but I want you to be wise as to what is good and innocent
as to what is evil (Romans 16:17-19).

A heretic (*haireticos*) is "a person who is a schismatic, who divides
a congregation with false teaching. Such a one is to be isolated
from the community" (Titus 3:10-11).[2] Ralph Earle said the word comes

from the verb meaning "to choose." So *haireticos* means "capable of choosing" and then "causing division." Josephus used this word for the three *haireseis* – Pharisees, Sadducees and Essenes, the sects of Judaism.[3] By its nature, heresy or false doctrine misleads and causes division. The Christian who loves the truth cannot tolerate what is false. He must separate himself from falsehood, or he will be swept away by its error.

What Is Error?

A person in error is a deceived person. The Greek term *plane* means "error, deception, deceit." In all the New Testament instances of *plane*, the word refers figuratively to moral (Romans 1:27) or spiritual (1 John 4:6) deception or error. Paul's appeal for maturity was so that people would no longer be deceived by error (Ephesians 4:14; 2 Peter 2:18; 3:17; Jude 11).[4] Louw and Nida describe error (*plane*) as the content of what misleads or deceives – "misleading belief, deceptive belief, error, mistaken view."[5] We hear many people claim that a person who is mistaken on some points is nonetheless spiritually acceptable to God. This position, however, runs solidly against the meaning of error. A person misled or mistaken on baptism, for instance, is still in error. Being mistaken does not justify a wrong practice. Being misled or mistaken does not turn sprinkling (*rhantizo*) into an action equivalent to immersing (*baptizo*). Although the latter is obedient to Scripture, the other is innovative error. Using the terms "mistaken" and "misled" does not turn a lie into the truth. We are all urged to be gracious and kind to those in error (Colossians 4:6; 2 Timothy 2:24-26); Christians have no place for being rude or ugly toward those outside the Body. But it is not kind to leave those outside the body of Christ with the erroneous impression they are all right with the Lord. To suggest God looks only at the heart and does not care about the practice of baptism ignores the point of Romans 6:16-18:

> Do you not know that if you present yourselves to anyone as obedient slaves, you are slaves of the one whom you obey, either of sin, which leads to death, or of obedience, which leads to righteousness? But thanks be to God, that

you who were once slaves of sin have become obedient from the heart to the standard of teaching to which you were committed, and, having been set free from sin, have become slaves of righteousness.

Paul argued that the Romans became obedient from the heart to "the standard of teaching to which [they] were committed." The heart does not release one from obeying forms. When the heart is filled with love, it induces one to obey with carefulness. This form (*tupon*) is an example or pattern that Paul thanked God the Romans followed. When they obediently committed themselves to follow Christ, they did it through these defined and understood patterns and examples. Earlier in Romans 6, Paul described baptism in terms of the burial and resurrection of Jesus from the dead. One died to sin and was freed from it in such a baptism (vv. 3-7). Paul's rhetorical question in verses 3-4 implies the pattern or example the people should have known and followed: "Do you not know that all of us who have been baptized into Christ Jesus were baptized into his death? We were buried therefore with him by baptism into death, in order that, just as Christ was raised from the dead by the glory of the Father, we too might walk in newness of life."

Neither sprinkling nor pouring fits this pattern of death, burial and resurrection that unites one with Christ. Immersion, on the other hand, easily fits the pattern and follows the example of Christ. At the time of this obedience, God graciously frees one from sin. Just as God raised up Jesus to have new life, so God raises Christians up to walk in newness of life. The new life follows the baptism; it does not precede it.

Those who inexcusably change baptism into a mere "act of obedi- ence after salvation" also skirt the common pattern Paul expected the Romans to understand. One did not find freedom from sin until one had new life. God raised Jesus up and gave Him new life, and God raises us up in baptism and gives us new life. When people embrace or tolerate a salvation by faith alone and without the obedience of baptism, they deny the commonly understood form or pattern of teaching that Paul expected the Romans to grasp. Such people pervert the gospel by shortchanging it.

Peter warned Christians about the untaught and unstable who distorted Paul's writings and the rest of the Scriptures to their own destruction.

He warned, "You therefore, beloved, knowing this beforehand, take care that you are not carried away with the error of lawless people and lose your own stability: But grow in the grace and knowledge of our Lord and Savior Jesus Christ" (2 Peter 3:17-18). Error brings about spiritual destruction and poses a real threat to those who fail to hold firmly to the truth. Peter expected Christians to leave error and to grow in their knowledge of the Lord and His will. The idea one may remain in error and still be pleasing to God is not considered. Christians must grow out of error or fall from God's grace (Galatians 5:4).

In like manner, the Holy Spirit through the writing of the epistle of James made a difference between truth and error. One cannot embrace error with impunity; there is such a thing as heresy. James 5:19-20 says, "My brothers, if any among you wanders from the truth and someone brings him back, let him know that whoever brings back a sinner from his wandering will save his soul from death and will cover a multitude of sins." Erring from the truth is spiritually destructive; it can cost a Christian his soul.

Interestingly, we are not told from which truth this "brother" has strayed. We are simply told he has strayed from the truth. J.W. Roberts makes this comment: "To wander from the truth is to be deceived (mistaken) and thus led away from the truth, the truth being the gospel of Jesus Christ. It is possible for one to deceive himself or be deceived by others." [6] Although some have no problem with being misled or deceived, James treats it seriously. The origin of this problem is found in the statement "wander from the truth" (James 5:19). The truth means, of course, the Word of God. "Your word is truth" (John 17:17). Unless the believer stays close to the truth, he will drift away. "Therefore we must pay much closer attention to what we have heard, lest we drift away from it" (Hebrews 2:1).

False Doctrine Is Evil

A person who teaches false doctrines either lies about God or about His will for humanity. All lying is evil and condemned (Revelation 21:8). What is often called "mistaken" is in reality deception. It is evil to deceive others (John 8:44). Lying to another by giving him or her false hope is cruel. Allowing people to remain deceived when the truth could lead them out of error is cruel and criminal, even by human terms (Ezekiel 3:18-21). A person who supports teaching false doctrines shares in their "wicked works" (2 John 10-11).

A person who leads others to believe a false doctrine also leads them into "more and more ungodliness" and may shipwreck their faith (2 Timothy 2:16-18; Titus 1:10-11). A person who presses a false belief or practice to the division of the church has committed great sin (Titus 3:10-11), such sin that will cause a person not to inherit the kingdom of God (Galatians 5:19-21).

Perverting the Gospel

What is the gospel? To hear some speak, the gospel is merely facts. They say that 1 Corinthians 15 makes it clear the gospel is comprised of the facts of the death, burial and resurrection of Jesus Christ. The Holy Spirit through Paul said:

> Now I would remind you, brothers, of the gospel I preached to you, which you received, in which you stand, and by which you are being saved, if you hold fast to the word I preached to you – unless you believed in vain. For I delivered to you as of first importance what I also received: that Christ died for our sins in accordance with the Scriptures, that he was buried, that he was raised on the third day in according with the Scriptures, and that he appeared to Cephas, then to the twelve (1 Corinthians 15:1-5).

• **First, the word gospel means "good news."** Good news is a message, not facts. This message was made known, preached and received. The early Christians took their stand on this message. They were saved by this message. They were expected to hold fast to the Word that was preached to remain saved. If they let go of the message, they believed in vain.

• **Second, the message of the apostles was persuasive.** They taught the message with an end in mind. They wanted their listeners to hear and to obey what they heard. "Knowing the fear of the Lord," they persuaded people (2 Corinthians 5:11). "Working together with him, then, we appeal to you not to receive the grace of God in vain" (6:1).

In Acts 18:4, Paul was reasoning in the synagogue every Sabbath and trying to persuade Jews and Greeks. Paul told Timothy:

> And the Lord's servant must not be quarrelsome but kind to everyone, able to teach, patiently enduring evil, correcting his opponents with gentleness. God may perhaps grant them repentance leading to a knowledge of the truth, and they may come to their senses and escape from the snare of the devil, after being captured by him to do his will (2 Timothy 2:24-26).

The belief that good news exists and demands no response is absurd.

• **Third, Paul sought and expected steadfast obedience to this message.** Obedience to the gospel was the goal (Romans 10:14; 2 Thessalonians 1:7-9; 1 Peter 4:17). Paul wanted those who believed the gospel to be obedient to the faith (Romans 1:5; 16:25-27; see also Acts 6:7). The power of the gospel worked when people believed and heeded that message. The gospel is God's power to save those who believe (Romans 1:16; 1 Corinthians 1:21). Let's not commit the fallacy of confusing the points of the message with the purpose of the message. The good news is a message of salvation to the one who hears and obeys.

Paul's strongest statement about false doctrine comes in Galatians 1:6-9. Some Jewish Christians were going beyond the gospel to demand that Gentile Christians keep the Old Testament Law as well as the teaching of the gospel. Paul said:

> I am astonished that you are so quickly deserting him who called you in the grace of Christ and are turning to a different gospel – not that there is another one, but there are some who trouble you and want to distort the gospel of Christ. But even if we or an angel from heaven should preach to you a gospel contrary to the one we preached to you, let him be accursed. As we have said before, so now I say again: If anyone is preaching to you a gospel contrary to the one you received, let him be accursed (Galatians 1:6-9).

There can be no doubt from Paul's language that false doctrines that pervert the gospel will condemn those who embrace them.

The Judaizers of the first century who sought to bind circumcision and the Law of Moses on Christians taught many other things right. There is no hint they denied the resurrection, denied the deity of Jesus, or contended for salvation before baptism. We have no reason to believe they contended for instrumental music in worship, sought to change the Lord's Supper, or believed in denominational Christianity. God condemned them for the wrong things they taught, although they held many things right. They taught a perverted gospel contrary to the gospel of Christ and were accursed for it.

In essence, false teachers have become lawless. They are acting outside the will and teaching of God. Distorting God's teaching is a crime against God; this distorted teaching disturbs the brethren and produces sand theology (Matthew 7:24-27). The Holy Spirit through Paul directed the young preacher Timothy to stay close to the Scriptures. Paul "renounced disgraceful, underhanded ways" and refused "to practice cunning or to tamper with God's word" (2 Corinthians 4:2). The cunning of the devil comes in his ability to distort the truth just enough to lead one into error. Rat poison is almost totally cornmeal. If it were not, it could not attract and fool the rats; but two percent poison is enough to kill them. False teachers realize they must approach the naive with what is mostly true; otherwise they could not fool them. A little lie, however, is still a lie and still dangerous.

Paul warned Timothy, "Until I come, devote yourself to the public reading of Scripture, to exhortation, to teaching. Keep a close watch on yourself and on the teaching. Persist in this, for by so doing you will save both yourself and your hearers" (1 Timothy 4:13, 16). Here again, the principle applies to teaching on any topic. If what one teaches does not matter, such language as Paul used in verse 16 is indeed absurd. Teaching does indeed affect one's salvation.

People Who Cause Division With Their Teaching

When a teacher begins spreading a destructive false doctrine, he affects many other people and disturbs the unity of a congregation or perhaps many congregations. The biblical warning "A little leaven leavens the whole lump" applies as readily to false teaching as it does to immoral behavior (Galatians 5:9; 1 Corinthians 5:6). Paul warned the Romans, "I appeal to you, brothers, to watch out for those who cause divisions and create obstacles contrary to the doctrine that you have been taught; avoid them. For such persons do not serve our Lord Christ, but their own appetites, and by smooth talk and flattery they deceive the hearts of the naive" (Romans 16:17-18). False teachers clearly not only ruin their own spiritual lives but also ruin those who believe them.

Paul instructed Titus to appoint elders in every city (Titus 1:5). An elder must meet some demanding qualifications:

> He must hold firm the trustworthy word as taught, so that he may be able to give instruction in sound doctrine and also to rebuke those who contradict it. For there are many who are insubordinate, empty talkers and deceivers, especially those of the circumcision party. They must be silenced, since they are upsetting whole families by teaching for shameful gain what they ought not to teach (Titus 1:9-11).

Clearly, false doctrine leads to the deception and the upsetting of whole families. These men had nothing of value to say and led others into rebellion and deception. Many people today claim to teach the truth but are merely peddlers of error. We live in a world filled with religious pseudo intellectuals who think they know the truth (1 Timothy 1:6-7). They know just enough to be dangerous. We must get over the false notion that being mistaken has no consequences. Lies lead to eternal damnation (John 8:44); only the truth leads to salvation (1 Timothy 2:3-4).

Consequently, Paul told Titus, "But avoid foolish controversies, genealogies, dissensions, and quarrels about the law, for they are unprofitable and worthless. As for a person who stirs up division, after warning him once and then twice, have nothing more to do with him, knowing that such a person is warped and sinful; he is self-condemned" (Titus 3:9-11). A factious (*hairetikos*) man is divisive, schismatic and heretical. He uses his false beliefs and ideas to drive a wedge among God's people. We must refuse to accept such people into our fellowship after a first and second warning because such men will corrupt the church.

Romans and Titus tell several things about schismatics in the church: (1) their motives are selfish; (2) they use deceitful means to influence the unsuspecting; (3) their teaching is contrary to the apostolic teaching; (4) they create dissensions and factions that split God's people; and (5) they are to be "watched," "turned away from," and "rejected."[8] Jimmy Jividen noted this about schismatics:

> Schismatics will be judged by God for their destructive behavior in the fellowship of the church. They also must be judged by the church itself. Those who cause division in the church must not be tolerated. The body of Christ must cut off any member who is divisive. If they do not, the body itself will be destroyed. Every church split could have been prevented if the church had excluded the schismatics from its fellowship before they formed a party.[9]

God values the purity of His church morally and doctrinally. Anyone who disturbs the peace and doctrinal purity of His people poses a threat to the unity for which Jesus prayed (John 17:20-23). God cannot look upon doctrinal sin with favor any more than He can look upon moral sin that way (Habakkuk 1:13).

Both Peter and Jude by inspiration spoke of the serious threat false teachers pose to the body of Christ (2 Peter 2:1-3; Jude 11-13, 17-19).

Testing the Spirits

John gave instruction to the early Christians who were facing challenges from a group that had left them, a group teaching error.

> Beloved, do not believe every spirit, but test the spirits to see whether they are from God, for many false prophets have gone out into the world. By this you know the Spirit of God: every spirit that confesses that Jesus Christ has come in the flesh is from God, and every spirit that does not confess Jesus is not from God. This is the spirit of the antichrist, which you heard was coming and now is in the world already (1 John 4:1-3).

Christians must not accept whatever they hear; they are to examine it and compare it to the truth.

The Scriptures regard the Bereans as noble; "they received the word with all eagerness, examining the Scriptures daily to see if these things were so" (Acts 17:11). Paul urged Timothy in 2 Timothy 2:15-18:

> Do your best to present yourself to God as one approved, a worker who has no need to be ashamed, rightly handling the word of truth. But avoid irreverent babble, for it will lead people into more and more ungodliness, and their talk will spread like gangrene. Among them are Hymenaeus and Philetus, who have swerved from the truth, saying that the resurrection has already happened. They are upsetting the faith of some.

The apostles were ever vigilant to evaluate teaching to keep others from leading brethren astray from the truth. They kept a close watch on others and on themselves to make sure they remained faithful to their calling (1 Timothy 4:16).

Make no mistake; the postmodernists among our brethren believe mainstream churches of Christ are guilty of "salvific judgmentalism" and will be lost like the Pharisees. In their eyes, we are legalistic, Pharisaical and lost because we insist on God's instructions about baptism as immersion, on the baptism of responsible and penitent believers, and on the purpose of baptism being the forgiveness of sin. In their eyes, churches of Christ have never understood the grace of God.

We have some among us today who are suggesting that biblical, Christian baptism is not necessary to salvation. They not only make this claim but also judge us for being narrow when we insist on doing things biblically. They see no reason to distinguish infant sprinkling from the immersion of a penitent believer; they believe both are saved.

An organist in a denominational church asked a postmodern minister in the churches of Christ if she should be baptized again – by immersion this time. She explained she had been sprinkled when she was a few weeks old. She asked, "Do you regard me as a Christian? Do you count me as your sister in Christ? Or do you think I am lost and need to be saved?" Here was his answer:

> Of course I see you as a Christian! And I'm sorry you have apparently met somebody from a Church of Christ or some

other immersionist group who treated you otherwise. Please judge me only for myself, all right? I understand the word "Christian" to mean "one who gives allegiance to Christ." And what you have just told me fairly screams your desire to honor him and do his will. While you and I probably won't see eye-to-eye on everything about the Christian religion – I can't even claim that for my wife and me – we certainly do see our faith in and love for Jesus to be at the heart of our identities.

So, yes I see the two of us as equals and peers. We are brother and sister to each other in the one great family or church of the Living God. We are sometimes-confused and always-inadequate believers who are trying to grow in our faith. We are both Christ-followers who want to be closer to the one we confess as our Lord.

And, no, I don't think you are lost. You are no "unbeliever" or "pagan" in my eyes. For someone such as me who believes a Christian can fall away from grace and be lost, let me be clear: I don't think that happens when a believer has a flaw in her theology or character. I believe people in Christ can be lost if they deliberately reject the truth and willfully sin against God. But for his grace to his children in our frailty, misinterpretations, and sins, not even one of us could have the hope of salvation.[10]

A close inspection of this answer shows that this postmodernist does not believe one must hear and obey the Lord. He believes that a mistaken, deceived understanding is as good as a true one. He argues that because we are human and frail, we do not need to have any true understanding about God's requirements in baptism. A mistaken sprinkling is as good as an educated immersion. A deceived infant sprinkling is as good as the immersion of a penitent believer. To him, a good heart removes the need to be obedient to God's voice. How did the response of a good but deceived heart get to be as valid in God's eyes as the response of a good and honest heart (Luke 8:11, 14)? How did a corrupted seed produce the same good as the true seed?

When considering baptism, have you ever stopped to ask who is active and who is passive? In baptism God is active, and we are passive. "Be baptized" is a passive imperative. It demands that we allow someone to act upon us. Physically, another person immerses us in water. Spiritually speaking, however, God is acting upon us (Colossians 2:12-13). In baptism God causes us to die to sin, immerses us in the death of Christ, forgives our sins, washes us clean, buries us with Christ, raises us up with Christ to walk in newness of life, adds us to His church, and causes our new birth so that we may enter the kingdom. In baptism, we are submitting to God's activity. We are responding to His gift of mercy and grace. To say that we do not need to be baptized to be saved is to interfere with God's activity in our lives. How dare anyone interfere with God!

Deafening Silence

Sociologists say that a cultural shift takes place every four to five years as a new generation comes along unexposed to the social forces of older adults. Many of the youngest adults can hardly remember when there were no cell phones, no cable companies and no computers. They have lived under a president named Bush, Clinton or Obama. The preaching in churches of Christ has changed in the last generation. Over time the church has become afraid to say much of anything with conviction. Preachers preach much love but little truth, much grace but little repentance, much salvation but little obedience, and much on relationships but little on relating responsibly to God Himself. Some speak much on believing and confuse their listeners by speaking little on what to believe.

It seems we have forgotten phrases like "the whole counsel of God" and have substituted "preach only positive" messages that make people feel good (Acts 20:27). Such substitution is unfaithful. It seems we have forgotten the instruction to "reprove" and to "rebuke" (2 Timothy 4:2). Our youngest adults in the church are confused by their leaders' constant apologizing, qualifying and "dumbing down." Leaders speak what we believe unless someone gets offended, and then (all of a sudden) we do not believe it enough to speak. No wonder they are confused. Young adults want conviction, and we give them apologies. Young adults are not afraid of the truth, but some cannot seem to bring themselves to admit what they believe. Our youngest adults are confused because their leaders have confused them with doublespeak and doubt in their own beliefs. Tragic!

Spineless leaders who will not speak their convictions have jettisoned their leadership to a chaotic culture. They have left a generation at the mercy of every wind that blows because they remain untaught. Their preaching will never set this generation free from sin or error. Only the truth can do that. I have watched a generation of our people lose their beliefs and question their most basic tenets. We can't say baptism is "for the remission of sins" because we know good immersed people who believe they were saved before baptism. We can't say baptism is immersion because we know good sprinkled folks. We can't speak against women leading in worship because some good women do it. We can't speak against instruments in worship because some good people use them.

Isn't God also good? When did people count more than God? When did we feel permitted to hush God and the Scriptures so that we do not offend anyone? A new generation feels little hesitance to tell God to hush. He is utterly disrespected, made common and demoted from His place as the one true and living God so that we might not offend people. What if God is offended at our silence? Doesn't God matter?

Blame It on the Spirit

For many years the evangelical world has believed the Holy Spirit worked directly on their hearts, not only in bringing about salvation but also in day-to-day guidance. Often one might see in religious literature phrases that suggest the Holy Spirit spoke directly to someone or impressed on his heart to follow a particular course. Even among churches of Christ, we are seeing churches turning from the truth to error, supposedly at the prompting of the Holy Spirit. An eldership recently wrote a letter to the members of the congregation explaining why they were going to use instrumental music in one of their worship services. They said:

> In the last few months we have been led by the Spirit to believe that as one of our tools we need to offer a second

service, a service which will include a blend of a cappella and instrumental music. We realize that this is a break from our tradition and that many of you are struggling with this, but we have witnessed the Spirit's great movement in the Wednesday evening college worship, a worship service with instrumental worship. Where God is moving, we seek to join Him, even if that entails some departure from our tradition. We believe Jesus gave us this pattern in John 5:19 ("The son can do nothing by himself; he can only do what he sees his Father doing"). … We have spent considerable time inquiring of God and feel led by His Spirit to pursue the goal we set forth for 2009 and to utilize the implementation of two services as one of the tools for reaching this goal. We ask you to walk with us as we strive to walk with God.[11]

It is indeed hard to imagine the Holy Spirit led these elders to act divisively by adding a worship they knew would violate the consciences of some. Although the elders recognized a cappella music as a tradition, they seemed oblivious that it was a divine tradition – a tradition of the Holy Spirit Himself. They ignored the example set by Christ and the Spirit; neither the Son nor the Holy Spirit would speak new teachings or make new practices unless instructed by the Father (John 12:49-50; 16:12-13).

Of course, the evidence for these elders' change was not what the Holy Spirit had caused to be written in Scripture but their own observations. They did not tell how they knew the Spirit was moving. We wonder how they knew the Spirit was moving on the college class in their use of the instrument when there is no record of any church in the first century using an instrument. Did they hear speaking in tongues as they did at the house of Cornelius or at Ephesus? Did they see miracles?

If the Holy Spirit guided the apostles into all the truth in the first century (and He did – John 16:13; this the promise of Jesus), why didn't the Spirit reveal the need to use the instrument in the New Testament? Why didn't members of the early church, which was guided into all truth, understand they were to use the instrument? Why are the members of the congregation being asked to rely on the findings of the elders but given no scriptural precedence for the practice? Those who are bringing the Spirit to bear into what they are doing often ignore the all-sufficiency of the Scriptures. They forget the Scriptures claim they are inspired and complete. "All Scripture is breathed out by God and profitable for teaching, for reproof, for correction, and for training in righteousness, that the man of God may be competent, equipped for every good work" (2 Timothy 3:16-17). If Christianity had all truth and was equipped for every good work in the first century, we will not see any new truth or need any further equipping in the 21st century. "All" and "every" mean "all" and "every," not "all" except when I feel moved.

People today are using phrases such as "the Spirit led me to … ," "the Holy Spirit impressed on my heart to … " or "the Spirit prompted me to … " to justify their own choices and directions. Such subjective assertions are often more a statement of what people desire than of what the Spirit has revealed. The argument that they use to justify the instrument is also the argument women who want to preach use to deny the teaching of 1 Corinthians 14:34 and 1 Timothy 2:10-11. It is the argument people use to try to reinvent Christianity.

The Holy Spirit is not in the innovation business. Jesus said, "When the Spirit of truth comes, he will guide you into all the truth, for he will not speak on his own authority, but whatever he hears he will speak, and he will declare to you the things that are to come" (John 16:13). The Holy Spirit only speaks and acts what He hears from the Father. We are now "to contend for the faith that was once for all delivered to the saints" and not innovate and reinvent Christianity (Jude 3). In the days of Jeremiah, some false prophets were always claiming to speak the word of the Lord. Jeremiah said:

> Thus says the LORD of hosts: "Do not listen to the words of the prophets who prophesy to you, filling you with vain hopes. They speak visions of their own minds, not from the mouth of the LORD. They say continually to those who despise the word of the LORD, 'It shall be well with you'; and to everyone who stubbornly follows his own heart, they say, 'No disaster shall come upon you.' " For who among them has stood in the

council of the LORD to see and to hear his word, or who has paid attention to his word and listened (Jeremiah 23:16-18)?

I did not send the prophets, yet they ran; I did not speak to them, yet they prophesied. But if they had stood in my council, then they would have proclaimed my words to my people, and they would have turned them from their evil way, and from the evil of their deeds (Jeremiah 23:21-22).

Jeremiah spoke of prophets who were convinced God had spoken to them, but the vision came from their own hearts and minds. God did not speak to them; they were not listening to God. They spoke out of their own imagination. To blame the Spirit and say He moved us to innovate, to originate our own beliefs and practices, is ignorant and dishonoring to the Holy Spirit. Do not blame the Spirit; obey the Spirit who spoke in Scripture (1 Thessalonians 4:8). Do not go beyond the teaching of Scripture. Only in this way will you imitate the Son and Spirit.

Questions

1. An eldership perceives that young adults are "turned off" by sermons that warn against apostasy and order the preacher to preach only "positive sermons" that will not offend anyone. What will be the likely direction of that congregation over time?

2. How can non-biblical approaches to human behavior, such as those found in secular psychology, serve to camouflage error?

3. How can true spirituality be distinguished from emotionalism?

4. How is the elevation of specialists, such as sociologists and counselors, similar to the development of the clergy system in the first centuries of the church?

CHAPTER 9

THE EMERGING
Church

Might I suggest to you, that if you are thirsty for insight on theology, that you not drink from the toilet even though there is water there. – Mark Driscoll [1]

Emergent doesn't have a position on absolute truth, or on anything for that matter. Do you show up at a dinner party with your neighbors and ask, "What's this dinner party's position on absolute truth?" No, you don't, because it's a non-sensical question. – Tony Jones, 2005 National Youth Workers Convention [2]

More and more Christians say the usual ways of "doing church" no longer resonate in a contemporary, postmodern culture. Seeking to fill the gap, a growing movement called "the emerging church" is developing new forms of worship and theological questioning for a new cultural context. – Kim Lawton [3]

When we make it sound like we have all the bolts screwed down tight and all the nails hammered in, and everything's all boxed up and we've got it all figured out, at that moment, I think we have stopped being faithful. – Brian McLaren [4]

The book of Judges describes seven distinct cycles of rebellion and commitment to the Lord God while the Israelites lived in the Promised Land. Judges appears as a tragic sequel to the book of Joshua when the people were committed to the Lord (Judges 2:7). When the generation of Joshua died, "there arose another generation after them who did not know the LORD or the work that he had done for Israel" (v. 10). Because Israel failed to drive the Canaanites out of the land (1:19, 21, 35), the new generation fell into idolatry (2:12), intermarried with the wicked Canaanites (3:5-6), failed to listen to their judges (2:17), and turned away from God after the judges died (v. 19). When the Israelites left God, the Lord punished them by allowing a military defeat and enslavement to another nation. In time Israel apologetically prayed for deliverance, and God raised up a judge who led them in defeating their oppressors. The book of Judges convincingly shows that the people of God are just one generation away from apostasy.

Peter Drucker, a well-respected management and business guru, wrote in his book *Post-Capitalist Society*:

> Every few hundred years in Western history there occurs a sharp transformation. Within a few short decades, society rearranges itself – its worldview; its basic values; its social and political structure; its arts; its key institutions. Fifty years later, there is a new world. And the people born then cannot even imagine the world in which their grandparents lived and into which their parents were born. We are living through just such a transition. [5]

 Many younger people have known only a postmodern, post-Christian world, and that mindset is normal to them. Those born into a postmodern, post-Christian world do not have the traditional atmosphere and soil to remember. They do not have strong biblical roots to return to. We should not expect postmoderns one day to "grow up" and become traditional Christians. They do not know how.

Postmodern Religion

The emerging church is a label that has been used to refer to a particular movement of religionists who are rethinking Christianity against the backdrop of postmodernism. Some have spoken of this movement more as a conversation between those who believe we must "do church" differently to reach a culture with a postmodern mindset. Mark Driscoll, a leader in this movement, says, "Wading through the entire emerging church milieu is incredibly complicated." He sees four lanes on the emerging church highway: emerging evangelicals, house church evangelicals, emerging reformers, and emergent liberals.

Driscoll says the first three categories, which compose most of the emerging church movement, commonly hold views that are theologically orthodox. They are not interested in reconsidering major Christian doctrines or morals. He regards the fourth lane, the emergent liberal, as the most controversial, and we are examining this lane. "The Emergent Liberal lane of the emerging church has drifted away from a discussion about how to contextualize timeless Christian truth in timely cultural ways and has instead come to focus on creating a new Christianity."[6] Emergent liberals range from the theological fringe of orthodoxy to heresy that questions or denies the authority of the Bible, the Trinity, the deity of Jesus Christ, the death of Jesus on the cross for our sins, and the exclusivity of Jesus as the way to heaven. Emergent liberals think hell is small and without torment and that we cannot know whether homosexuality or fornication is a sin. Driscoll says emergent liberals see little conversion growth but rather gather "disgruntled Christians and people intrigued by false doctrine."[7] Emergents such as Brian McLaren skirt the truth and are fuzzy about what they believe.

Knowing the Times

We must understand the times and pray to God for wisdom. We need some sons of Issachar today, some mighty men who know how to win the war for God with sound, strategic thinking. First Chronicles 12:32 says the sons of Issachar were men who understood the times, with knowledge of what Israel should do.

The emerging church movement is made up of many diverse elements. Not all emerging adherents believe alike or act alike. Therefore, we do not wish to overstate the case. Some embrace classic liberalism whereas others remain conservative. Some race to ancient forms of worship and contemplative prayer. Others abandon traditional worship in favor of conversations and visits to a museum or a park. Many emergents want to "experience" God with all five senses. At this point the emerging church movement is a hodgepodge of sometimes contradictory ideas united by a rejection of modern fundamentalism. Emergents feel such certainty found in modern belief causes one to be arrogant and to exert manipulative power over others. Because they are sure no one can be certain of absolute truth, they feel free to embrace religious pluralism and to despise judgmentalism.

The postmodern mindset rejects modern rationalism, objective truth and absolutes. Some emergents have oddly grown close to classic, liberal theology and embrace the teachings of higher criticism. Some no longer regard the Scriptures as verbally inspired, inerrant or authoritative in their original intent. They believe the authority of Scripture arises from how the reader lives out the message in a postmodern context. They believe how they see Scripture is more true than how the writers of Scripture (who were inspired by the Holy Spirit) intended for Scripture to be understood.

In *The Church on the Other Side,* McLaren argues that because we have a new world we "need a new church." [8] He regards everyone as a pilgrim who is always searching but never arriving. He believes we should get over our hang-up with absolute truth and be more pluralistic. He says we need to get rid of the modernistic views of inerrancy and the uniquely absolute significance of Jesus Christ as the only way to salvation. For him the emerging church must be open, flexible and pluralistic.

This view, however, flies in the face of the Holy Spirit's instructions through Paul to the church in Colossae that also found cultural clashes. The Bible says:

> Therefore, as you received Christ Jesus the Lord, so walk in him, rooted and built up in him and established in the faith, just as you were taught, abounding in thanksgiving. See to it that no one takes you captive by philosophy and empty deceit, according to human tradition, according to the

elemental spirits of the world, and not according to Christ (Colossians 2:6-8).

Why then would emergents feel so strongly about changing "church"? Emergents believe that they have been gifted to re-create how to "do Christianity" for the coming generation. They are drawing their conviction to change from their gut feelings and from their belief the Holy Spirit is leading them to do this. Concentrating on what they consider to be defects in the church as it has been passed down to them, they feel called to reshape Christianity in ways that appeal to the diverse, skeptical culture of our time.

Emergents often quote 1 Corinthians 9:19-23 to justify their new ways of "doing church." Emergents have a smorgasbord outlook where individuals choose for themselves what they want and piece together their own theological and devotional practices like a diner would put together his salad at a salad bar. Some of their selected items, however, have nothing to do with Christianity and everything to do with current culture.

Although Paul sought to identify with the cultures in which he lived (1 Corinthians 9:19-23), he kept his focus on standing in the apostolic traditions he received (11:1; 15:1-3). To suggest somehow that he wanted to reinvent or re-create Christianity to fit a pagan world contradicts his clear stands on the truth. Among pagans or Jews, Paul understood that he was under the law of Christ. To him, Christian essentials were not negotiable. He identified with the groups only to the extent he could bring them into subjection to the Lord. Although removed a generation out of Palestine and into a fleshly and pagan culture at Corinth, he did not suggest a "reimagined" faith for a new generation. He held to what he received. "I have become all things to all people, that by all means I might save some. I do it all for the sake of the gospel, that I may share with them in its blessings" (9:22-23). He did not make the gospel bend to please them. He bent himself to lead people to the unchangeable gospel.

The Holy Spirit directs, "Do not be conformed to this world, but be transformed by the renewal of your mind, that by testing you may discern what is the will of God, what is good and acceptable and perfect" (Romans 12:2). Inspired, Paul wrote this from Corinth to the brethren at Rome. He did not encourage the brethren to conform to Roman standards but rather to change their lives into conformity with the will of God. He wanted them to prove in their lives the will of God was good and acceptable and perfect. The Romans did not need to re-create moral or spiritual lives to fit the culture; they needed to transform their lives so the culture could see the superiority of Christianity to paganism. When emergents desert Christ's eternal Word to connect to culture, they lose the foundation of their faith (Matthew 7:24-27). They may lead someone somewhere, but the house they build is likely built on sand.

Emergents see little need for orthodoxy (believing the right doctrines) but stress orthopraxy (living the right life). They believe if you live the right life, you will have the right doctrine. Some believe that doctrine is not false unless it also has some immoral lifestyle to go with it. For them, the need for "true" doctrine is a divisive stumbling block. Connecting and reaching out are more important to them than pressing one belief over another. Orthopraxy, in their thinking, has less to do with sexual morals and more to do with kindness toward others. They do not judge the sexually immoral but are harsh toward those who are judgmental.

God and His Word

Some emergents are unwilling, for instance, to put Jesus above other religions. McLaren, an emerging church leader, said,

> I don't believe making disciples must equal making adherents to the Christian religion. It may be advisable in many (not all!) circumstances to help people become followers of Jesus and remain within their Buddhist, Hindu or Jewish contexts … rather than resolving the paradox via pronouncements on the eternal destiny of people more convinced by or loyal to other religions than ours, we simply move on. … To help Buddhists, Muslims, Christians, and everyone else experience life to the full in the way of Jesus (while learning it better myself), I would gladly become one of them (whoever

they are, to whatever degree I can, to embrace them, to join them, to enter into their world without judgment but with saving love as mine has been entered by the Lord.[9]

I don't hope all Jews or Hindus will become members of the Christian religion. But I do hope all Jews or Hindus will become Jewish or Hindu followers of Jesus.[10]

More recently, McLaren called for emergents to join with their Muslim friends during their fast in celebration of Ramadan. He explains:

We, as Christians, humbly seek to join Muslims in this observance of Ramadan as a God-honoring expression of peace, fellowship, and neighborliness. Each of us will have at least one Muslim friend who will serve as our partner in the fast. These friends welcome us in the same spirit of peace, fellowship, and neighborliness. We will seek to avoid being disrespectful or unfaithful to our own faith tradition in our desire to be respectful to the faith tradition of our friends. For example, since the Bible teaches us the importance of fasting and being generous to the poor, we can participate as Christians in fidelity to the Bible as our Muslim friends do so in fidelity to the Quran.[11]

One must wonder why to connect with pagans Paul did not call for Christians to join in the idolatrous celebrations of the time as a God-honoring expression of peace. Instead the Holy Spirit spoke clearly through Paul:

Do not be unequally yoked with unbelievers. For what partnership has righteousness with lawlessness? Or what fellowship has light with darkness? What accord has Christ with Belial? Or what portion does a believer share with an unbeliever? What agreement has the temple of God with idols? For we are the temple of the living God; as God said, "I will make my dwelling among them and walk among them, and I will be their God, and they shall be my people. Therefore go out from their midst, and be separate from them, says the Lord, and touch no unclean thing; then I will welcome you, and I will be a father to you, and you shall be sons and daughters to me, says the Lord Almighty" (2 Corinthians 6:14-18).

Emergents who do not consider the Lord God of heaven as exclusive will not hold to the Bible exclusively either. Many emergents disparage the Bible as the unique authority over the lives of Christians. Neil Livingstone, an emerging church leader, said:

> The truth of the Bible, like any truth, is not best seen "objectively." … Where then can I find authority that I can be sure of? Since God is (by and large) invisible, we are left with ordinary people holding a book. As we had said before, we cannot simply "go to the book." Truth cannot properly reside as a mere proposition on a paper. Truth lives in persons and relationships.[12]

Another emerging author, Stanley Hauerwas, recently argued,

> The reformation doctrine of *sola scriptura*, joined to the invention of the printing press and underwritten by the democratic trust in the intelligence of the "common person," has created the situation that now makes people believe that they can read the Bible "on their own." That presumption must be challenged, and that is why the Scripture should be taken away from Christians in North America.[13]

Interestingly, Hauerwas assumes he has enough wisdom to say Christians in North America should not read the Bible on their own. He assumes he knows the proper way to pursue religion but denies others the right.

Alan Jones, an Episcopal priest in San Francisco, spoke of what he calls "authentic" Christianity in terms of lifestyle but without biblical doctrine.

> I am no longer interested, in the first instance, in what a person believes. Most of the time it's so much clutter in the brain. … I wouldn't trust an inch many people who profess a belief in God. Others who do not or who doubt have won my trust. I want to know if joy, curiosity, struggle, and compassion bubble up in a person's life. I'm interested in being fully alive. There is no objective authority.[14]

This thinking from Jones' book *Reimagining Christianity* is what McLaren quotes and endorses.

Dealing With Sin

Emergents often refuse to judge anyone (except conservative Christians) for any reason. They doubt whether there is such a thing as sin. They regard as heroes and "good guys" anyone who refuses to label homosexuality or abortion as sin. They speak much of the grace of Christ but willingly forget Jesus repeatedly called people to repentance (Matthew 4:17). Many emergents have a theology that does not care whether people continue to commit sin. They assume because they see little wrong with abortion or homosexuality that God feels the same way. In their minds, grace covers it all, whether they regard it wrong or not. Mark Driscoll tells of interviewing emergent liberal Doug Pagitt during a conference in Seattle in 2007. Driscoll asked, "Is homosexuality an acceptable practice for a Christian?" Pagitt answered plainly, "Yes." [15]

McLaren believes sermons about doctrine, sin and salvation create factions and should be replaced with messages about global issues. He believes many TV and radio evangelists preach the fear-mongering and finger-pointing messages that promote factionalism. McLaren proposed that preaching should repair, rather than incite, controversial issues. These include poverty and climate change, and he encouraged his audience not to shy away from such global issues. He said, "We can't really afford to waste too many Sundays with so much at stake." [16] One blogger at a postmodern site wrote, "In a post-Christian, postmodern world aren't sermons an absolute waste of time?" [17] Another blogger said, "I agree with you … that the construction of escaping the earth and going to heaven is, 'shallow, self-seeking and dehumanizing.'" [18]

Emergents believe in the process of "diaprax" or "dialogue searching for consensus." When the Word of God is dialogued (as opposed to being taught didactically) between believers and unbelievers, and consensus is reached – agreement that all are comfortable with – then emergents have achieved their goal. "Unfortunately, this message waters down the Word of God and conditions the participants to accept (and even celebrate) their compromise. This new synthesis becomes the starting thesis for the next meeting. The fear of alienation from the group is the pressure that prevents an individual from standing firm for the truth of the Word of God. The fear of man then overrides the fear of God." [13]

For the emerging church, reaching out is more important than keeping. They believe their mission is to reach out to the unchurched and unbelieving culture. They believe their methods are the right means to their mission. Members of churches who question or resist the new changes the leader is imposing are reprimanded and usually asked to leave. Emerging believers reject any posture that hints at exclusivism except when the dissenters are conservatives. Dogmatic Christians are not treated as kindly in the conversation as others are. They are told to get with the program or get out. Members who disagree with emergent leaders are expendable; leaders would rather reach out than keep dissidents. A moderator at the Postmodern_Theology website said, "If you are a 'modern' (as opposed to a postmodern) believer and desire to 'fix' us, we suggest you join another group where such is welcomed." Postmoderns are tolerant of everything except conviction. They hate finger-pointing unless they are the ones doing it.

Hell

Things such as sin, repentance and hell have little place in the emerging church. Because there are no moral absolutes, emergents cannot be sure that they can criticize anything or that God will cause anyone to be lost. Hell is as small as can be, and almost no one is going there. Preaching against sin is fear-mongering and finger-pointing behavior that makes people feel uncomfortable. One cannot connect with others by critiquing, so we must not judge. Emergents do not believe Jesus died on the cross with salvation from hell on His mind; however Jesus talked more about hell than anyone. To suggest, as emergents do, that hell is not a significant matter rips the purpose of the cross out of the gospel. Emergents do not like the thought of hell. Even the thought of conditional immortality (the view that people will burn up and cease to exist in hell) is distasteful. Their rejection of hell is an example of their willingness to reject the teaching of the Lord for a religion they desire.

How Do We Address These Changes?

We cannot expect churches of Christ to be free from postmodern and evangelical, emerging church influence. Some among us are already excited about this new wave of spirituality found in worldly compromise, tolerance, candles and incense. Some of our bookstores are already filled with books supporting the emerging agenda. The emerging church movement has clearly chosen the broad way. Emergents have stepped into self-made religion that dismisses the Word and the will of God. They have denied Jesus His place as the one true Lord of all the earth. All of this they have done in the name of tolerance. Such tolerance pretends love, but love that lacks correction is empty-headed. We cannot hide our heads in the sand.

• **First, we must hold fast to what we believe.** What we believe does determine how Jesus relates to us (John 8:31-32). We hold fast to faith, hope and love. We do not stop speaking the exclusive nature of Jesus or deny there is one body. We do not forget who we are, whose we are, from where we have come, and where we are going. We hold fast to the teaching of Jesus Christ on sin, heaven, hell, salvation and morals. Paul provided the model for living in a hostile culture when he recalled, "not being outside the law of God but under the law of Christ" (1 Corinthians 9:21).

• **Second, we must live out our faith without apology.** Non-Christians need to see Christians prove that God's will is "good and acceptable and perfect" (Romans 12:2). We live convicted lives with love. We will not win everyone, but we will survive. We try to understand those with whom we must live (1 Chronicles 12:32) but do not conform to them (Romans 12:2). We identify with others but never lose focus of our place as sons of God (2 Corinthians 6:14-18). We show love to all, patience with those who are in error (2 Timothy 2:24-26), and a truthful kindness that does not end in false hope. We preach the truth that sets men free rather than wallow in a sentimentality that leaves one in sin.

• **Third, we recognize the inspired message as eternal not temporal (Jude 3).** God gave this faith for all people in all places for all time. God designed His divine kingdom to be eternal and not a human organization to be reinvented in succeeding generations (Luke 1:33). The Lord Jesus is the only King of His kingdom, and only He has a

116 • *A Faith Built on Sand*

right to make the rules. Because our Savior promised to guide the apostles into "all the truth" in the first century (John 16:13), we deny the need for new truth. Because God spoke for all time, what He said is as binding on us today as it was in the first century. The notion of God-gifted reinvention for a new culture makes God subject to men because He has changed to meet their needs.

God is the absolute Sovereign; He is not subject to man. Man is subject to Him. It is rebellion to think we should reinvent God's ways. This view proclaims God was not wise enough to design a universal faith. This view is more than inaccurate; it lacks trust in God. We look to an eternal God who transcends cultural shifts that are destined to die. Our commitment is to New Testament Christianity, not to modern or postmodern assumptions. We feel confident we can speak what the Lord speaks; we can believe what He teaches. Truth, logic and confidence in God's Word existed before either modernism or postmodernism came on the scene. While on earth, our Lord said, "It is written ... " (Matthew 4:4, 6, 10); and that firmly settled the matter. For Him, the Scripture cannot be broken (John 10:35). Jesus took pains to deliver the Father's message faithfully, to speak only and accurately what He heard from His Father (12:48-50). He did not dare to speak on His own initiative. We see no justification for thinking we can "re-create" the church for a postmodern generation. The church does not belong to us; it never has.

• **Fourth, we must once again see the utter uniqueness of Jesus as the one and only Lord.** Let us proclaim the reasons we believe in Him as the Lord and the Christ. Our pulpits must once again ring with evidences for faith, hope and love. Jesus is not just another holy man or moral leader. He is not just one voice among the many; He is the only way to God. He alone was raised from the dead; He alone sits on the throne at the right hand of God; and He alone will one day judge the world (Acts 2:32-36; 17:30-31).

• **Fifth, let us live with hope.** We must live as people born again to a new life in a world bound for futility and confusion. Postmodern confusion has nothing to offer better than Christ. Just as generations came back to God in the Old Testament, so there will be returns to the one and only faith of all time (Jude 3). That it may take time should not cause us despair. The Lord is still on the throne, and His hand is with His people. The faith of the Scriptures has survived every challenge, and it will survive this one too.

• **Sixth, we must appeal to postmodern people with our biblical lives.** New Testament Christianity has always been countercultural. It loved when others were apathetic or hateful. It reached out when others did not see the need. It kept its conscience when others destroyed themselves morally. It did not compromise when the world called for compromise. True disciples are authentic not phony, genuine not superficial. They do not excuse their failures by a contrived, connection agenda. They connect by being true to Scripture, true to the Lord and true to their faith. They live their faith and live their love (James 2:14-18; 1 John 3:16-18). They do not apologize for their commitment to Christ, to truth, or to morality because they realize the Lord's way yields peace and the abundant life (John 10:10; James 3:13-18).

• **Seventh, we must continue to worship in spirit and in truth.** A substantive difference exists between evangelizing lost souls (which leads to an eternal difference) and merely cleaning up a park (which is an end in itself). A substantive difference exists between offering from our hearts a sacrifice of praise through "the fruit of our lips" (Hebrews 13:15) and admiring someone's art. A considerable difference exists between praising God according to His instructions in the New Testament and "doing church" according to our own desires. A great difference exists between choosing to worship in ways that honor God and "reinventing" church with the agenda to slap at the boring way our parents worshiped. The first way honors God; the second way arises from disgruntled people who are more concerned with what they don't want than with what honors God.

We worship God the Father because He is the only one worthy of our worship. We do not worship to honor our culture or any other, for that would be idolatry. When cultural desires and norms dictate what we do in worship more than divine, biblical instruction, we are worshiping ourselves. What gift is that to God? How honored does He feel? Isn't pressing our own agendas in worship more an act of disrespecting than honoring? The emerging church has set its agenda as an automatic reaction to boring, rigid parents. They want the freedom to develop new worship forms and "experience" God, but God has already revealed how He wants us to worship and relate to Him in the Scriptures. Our focus should be on pleasing Him, not reinventing what we do at church.

Questions

1. How is the cycle of apostasy found in the book of Judges like the history of the churches of Christ in the 19th and 20th centuries?

2. When the Lord's church uses materials drawn from the emerging church movement in teaching teenagers and young adults, what will be the likely outcome?

3. The emerging church movement is more experience-centered than truth-centered. What should a congregation do to prevent this sort of emphasis from being a springboard to apostasy?

4. Why is much contemporary religion hyper-zealous toward some good deeds, such as doing acts of benevolence, but apathetic toward other aspects of Christian living, such as sobriety or sexual purity?

CHAPTER 10

SYNTHETIC
Christianity

You shall not sow your vineyard with two kinds of seed, lest the whole yield be forfeited, the crop that you have sown and the yield of the vineyard. You shall not plow with an ox and a donkey together. You shall not wear cloth of wool and linen mixed together (Deuteronomy 22:9-11).

And the incense that you shall make according to its composition, you shall not make for yourselves. It shall be for you holy to the LORD. Whoever makes any like it to use as perfume shall be cut off from his people (Exodus 30:37-38).

There is one body and one Spirit – just as you were called to the one hope that belongs to your call – one Lord, one faith, one baptism, one God and Father of all, who is over all and through all and in all (Ephesians 4:4-6).

The word "synthetic" first appeared in 1916, and Webster's defines it as "something resulting from synthesis rather than occurring naturally, especially a product (as a drug or plastic) of chemical synthesis." Synthesizing is the act of mixing or blending various elements to create something new and different. The synthesis of many physical matters has blessed mankind. Where would we be without plastic? But when men blend the pure will of God with their own desires, they cannot help producing a hybrid never intended by God. The divine message authoritatively speaks to men. It is inspired, holy and sacred. It came from an all-knowing Being whose wisdom has never failed and whose Word is altogether righteous.

> Oh, the depth of the riches and wisdom and knowledge of God! How unsearchable are his judgments and how inscrutable his ways! "For who has known the mind of the Lord, or who has been his counselor? Or who has given a gift to him that he might be repaid?" For from him and through him and to him are all things. To him be glory forever. Amen (Romans 11:33-36).

The Loss of the Sacred

People are willing to synthesize their faith when they lose their sense of the sacred. If modern man denied God, postmodern man dismisses him. He has treated God as trivial and common. Postmodern man has little sense of the difference between the sacred and the profane. To blend the sacred with the profane unalterably corrupts our understanding of the Almighty. God is perfect in holiness, in love and in righteousness. Anytime a person attempts to blend in his faith the imperfections of humanity with the perfection of God, he will undoubtedly end up in error.

Aaron, fearing the disappearance of Moses, fell to the pressure from doubting Israel. They asked him to make them a god who would go before them. They had forgotten the Lord. When Aaron made the golden calf, the people said:

> "These are your gods, O Israel, who brought you up out of the land of Egypt!" When Aaron saw this, he built an altar before it. And Aaron made proclamation and said, "Tomorrow shall be a feast to the LORD." And they rose up early the next day and offered burnt offerings and brought peace offerings. And the people sat down to eat and drink and rose up to play (Exodus 32:4-6).

Calling a molten calf "the Lord" did not make it the God who delivered the Israelites from Egypt. Blending the human with the divine perverted their understanding. With a humanly contrived god, the people ate, drank and "rose up to play" (Exodus 32:6). In an inspired comment on this event, Paul said the people "desire[d] evil" (1 Corinthians 10:6). They actually rejoiced in "the works of their hands" (Acts 7:41). The people not only defiled their worship but also acted coarsely with their lascivious dancing (Exodus 32:19). The Hebrew verb *sahaq*, translated "play" in Exodus 32:6, is highly suggestive of sexual activities. The same verb is used in Genesis 26:8 and translated "caressing" in the New American Standard Bible. Considering the drinking that was taking place and the nakedness, the worship of the calf may have turned into a drunken sex orgy (Exodus 32:25; "out of control," NASB; "naked," KJV) that was not uncommon among the pagans. Perhaps some Israelites had picked up these ways of worshiping while they were slaves of the Egyptians. For whatever reason, their corrupted view of God led to lewd behavior.

Hundreds of years later, King Jotham reigned over Judah (750-732 B.C.). The Scriptures summarize his spiritual life in 2 Kings 15:34-35: "'And he did what was right in the eyes of the LORD, according to all that his father Uzziah had done. Nevertheless, the high places were not removed. The people still sacrificed and made offerings on the high places." Jotham held to God himself, except where the high places were concerned. He gave in to the people. Jotham's failure to stand against the idolatry at the high places opened the door of full-blown idolatry for his son Ahaz. When one generation compromises by allowing sin to co-exist with God, the next generation falls headlong into apostasy.

Ahaz "walked in the way of the kings of Israel. He even burned his son as an offering, according to the despicable practices of the nations whom the LORD drove out before the people of Israel. And he sacrificed and made offerings on the high places and on the hills and under every green tree" (2 Kings 16:3-4). Ahaz's sinful example brought about a lack of restraint in Judah; he was "very unfaithful to the LORD" (2 Chronicles 28:19). His full embrace of idolatry led him to trivialize God. When Rezin the king of Syria and Pekah the son of Remaliah, king of Israel threatened Judah, Ahaz gave in to their impotent threats and called to Tiglath-pileser, king of Assyria, to "rescue" Judah (2 Kings 16:7). When the king of Assyria captured Damascus, Ahaz went there to meet him.

Becoming enamored with an idolatrous altar at Damascus, King Ahaz sent the pattern of the altar to Uriah the priest and demanded he build one just like it and place it in the temple (2 Kings 16:10). Unfaithful Uriah did so. Incredibly, Uriah never questioned whether God would approve such an altar and never opposed Ahaz in the building of this idolatrous object.

> And when the king came from Damascus, the king viewed the altar. Then the king drew near to the altar and went up on it and burned his burnt offering and his grain offering and poured his drink offering and threw the blood of his peace offerings on the altar. And the bronze altar that was before the LORD he removed from the front of the house, from the place between his altar and the house of the LORD, and put it on the north side of his altar (2 Kings 16:12-14).

It did not occur to Ahaz he had supplanted God, and this is the case with most synthesizers. They think they can improve on God; they have a better way. Ahaz did not do away with the bronze altar; he merely made it trivial, except when he wanted to inquire by it (2 Kings 16:15). In his mind, his altar was better for the day-to-day offerings.

Although Ahaz is to blame for the blending of the human with the sacred, we must hold Uriah accountable for saying and doing nothing. He allowed the king to overrule God and introduce an additional human altar that God never authorized. Uriah proved faithless by remaining quiet and not speaking up for the Lord's altar. Today's preachers and elders who remain quiet and conciliatory while the wolf tears up the flock prove as worthless as Uriah.

In contrast, Azariah the priest with another 80 priests who were valiant men stood firm against King Uzziah of Judah. When Uzziah's heart became strong and proud, he "was unfaithful to the LORD his God and entered the temple of the LORD to burn incense on the altar of incense" (2 Chronicles 26:16). The priests opposed him and said, "It is not for you, Uzziah, to burn incense to the LORD, but for the priests, the sons of Aaron who are consecrated to burn incense. Go out of the sanctuary, for you have done wrong, and it will bring you no honor from the LORD God" (v. 18). Uzziah with his censer in his hand became enraged at the priests. In his heart he was as good as anybody; he did not have to mind the rules! God had been with him in the battle, and he thought he could worship in the temple like a priest if he wanted. Those who push man-made ways often think they are the specially gifted and do not have to mind the rules God really gave. Azariah the priest stood firm, however, against Uzziah the king.

God humbled King Uzziah. Only priests could offer incense; those in the tribe of Judah were excluded. They could not be priests, even if they were kings. "And King Uzziah was a leper to the day of his death, and being a leper lived in a separate house, for he was excluded from the house of the LORD. And Jotham his son was over the king's household, governing the people of the land" (2 Chronicles 26:21). God did not put up with Uzziah's corrupt and presumptuous attempt to worship in his own way. It is absurd to think God will put up with such today. No one can synthesize God's will with his or her will. No matter how good we think we are, we still fall short of a perfect God whose wisdom is limitless.

Diluting the Truth

Many people today think nothing of synthesizing an addition into the will of God. They believe in immersion as God's way, but they contend the human invention of sprinkling for baptism will work just as well. They believe one can righteously sing a cappella, but they see no problem with adding the innovation of instrumental music. They believe one is baptized so that God will forgive his sins, but they reason a deceived person who is baptized because his sins are already forgiven is doing God's will. (We still wonder how one is doing the will of God with a baptism that openly contradicts the truth. Those who confess a baptism that follows salvation are certainly depending upon a different baptism than what Peter proclaimed at Pentecost.) They believe in baptizing a penitent believer, but they also hold to a human tradition by regarding an unbelieving infant as a sufficient candidate for baptism. In their minds God does not care! We can edit God if we choose. We must not assume we can act in the silence of God. Uzziah's example proves God does notice; we cannot act on our own authority. We cannot add into God's menu our own spices and expect God to be pleased. We cannot get so good and so close to God that we are privileged to act presumptuously. "Among those who are near me I will be sanctified, and before all the people I will be glorified" (Leviticus 10:3).

God does not "gift" people to act on their own authority and reinvent the church. He gave His perfect will and all the truth in the first century to all people in all places for all time. He expects people to show their love for Him by keeping His commandments (John 14:15), not rewriting them for succeeding generations. God has not changed His mind about what is right and what is wrong. Sin is still sin. As humans, rather than debate or edit God's Word with cultural mores, should we not humble ourselves in His presence and accept His will for our lives? As advanced as society is, we still are not smarter or wiser than God. We may think we are quite wise because we "understand" the culture of our day. We may boast of our successful religiosity. We may even convince ourselves we are more compassionate and righteous than God's stated will because we refuse to be judgmental on moral and doctrinal differences. The human spirit has a thousand ways to convince itself it can do as it pleases.

The Need for Humility

After all the discussion, we must come to understand that we are limited humans. We do not know everything; we do not even know most things. We are not wise enough to outthink God or to correct His stated will for all people. We are strong on pride but short on wisdom. We may think we are "gifted," but we are not called to invent new churches. We are called to be faithful and to obey. If pride does anything, it robs us of our Christian usefulness. God cannot use the person who thinks he can synthesize God's will with his own to accommodate the new spiritual environment. In synthesis, the perfect will of God is ruined by human ignorance and foolishness. God wants a person "poor in spirit" who will take the divine will as it stands and transform his own life into conformity with that which is "good and acceptable and perfect" (Matthew 5:3; Romans 12:2). God's Word remains all-sufficient.

People always think they are right. Conflict usually arises when two parties think they are in the right yet disagree. In such cases, at least one of the two is wrong. Both may be wrong, but at least one is definitely wrong. Nobody likes to admit he is wrong because it is humiliating. To not humiliate and offend, postmodernists agree to ignore God's standards and claim everyone is right. No one goes home sobbing. From this removal of rigid standards, the synthesizer feels free to re-negotiate the plan of salvation, worship, and the organization of the church. He can allow his own ingredients to dominate the recipe and bake something new. He thinks he has really done something to help mankind religiously. Isaiah said,

> Seek the LORD while he may be found; call upon him while he is near; let the wicked forsake his way, and the unrighteous man his thoughts; let him return to the LORD, that he may have compassion on him, and to our God, for he will abundantly pardon. For my thoughts are not your thoughts, neither are your ways my ways, declares the LORD. For as the heavens are higher than the earth, so are my ways higher than your ways and my thoughts than your thoughts" (Isaiah 55:6-9).

Isaiah argues there is a substantial difference between our ways and God's ways. If we interject our thinking into God's, we necessarily fool ourselves with our own arrogance. We do not make God's ways or God's thoughts better by editing them.

The Arrogance of Correcting God

In reality, the "reinventor" of church has corrupted the perfect and crafted a hybrid religion. He has made a church after his own likeness, using little of God's wisdom and mostly his own. He has forgotten the proverb: "There is a way that seems right to a man, but its end is the way to death" (Proverbs 14:12). Jeremiah said, "I know, O LORD, that the way of man is not in himself, that it is not in man who walks to direct his steps" (Jeremiah 10:23). God has not summoned us to counsel Him. He does not need our foolishness; we need His wisdom. Synthesized religion has no respect for sacred wisdom because it assumes it can blend the divine with the human, the sacred with the profane.

Alloyed metals may be stronger, but one cannot alloy the faith without serious negative consequences. The book of Galatians speaks of the Judaizing Christians who sought to bind the Law of Moses on Gentile converts. They thought they could take elements of the old covenant and blend them into the new covenant. They did not strengthen their faith; they perverted it. Paul wrote:

> I am astonished that you are so quickly deserting him who called you in the grace of Christ and are turning to a different gospel – not that there is another one, but there are some who trouble you and want to distort the gospel of Christ. But even if we or an angel from heaven should preach to you a gospel contrary to the one we preached to you, let him be accursed. As we have said before, so now I say again: If anyone is preaching to you a gospel contrary to the one you received, let him be accursed (Galatians 1:6-9).

Paul was surprised anyone would consider another gospel other than the one he preached and they received. To change this gospel is to distort it, not help it. It loses power rather than gains powers. One cannot improve on God's revealed will, and Paul said anyone who tries does so to the cursing of his soul. Paul defended his gospel with this statement: "For I would have you know, brothers, that the gospel that was preached by me is not man's gospel. For I did not receive it from any man, nor was I taught it, but I received it through a revelation of Jesus Christ" (Galatians 1:11-12).

When people attempt to mix culture into the gospel, they weaken it. Although they may think they have made it more appealing to the masses, they rob it of its power. The Holy Spirit said through Paul: "Look: I, Paul, say to you that if you accept circumcision, Christ will be of no advantage to you. I testify again to every man who accepts circumcision that he is obligated to keep the whole law. You are severed from Christ, you who would be justified by the law; you have fallen away from grace" (Galatians 5:2-4). Rather than strengthen their faith, the Judaizers destroyed their relationship with Christ. They severed themselves from Christ and fell from grace. Thinking they were better than Paul by improving the gospel (in their minds), they lost their relationship with Christ.

Selective Obedience

Those who mix culture with the gospel prove themselves selective. They want the blessings and promises of the gospel without the responsibility. Some among us have bought into the foolish notion that the primary things of the gospel represent all that needs to be known. Quoting 1 Corinthians 15:1-5, they say the gospel is good news, a message to be preached. If one mentions a response to the gospel, they arrogantly object. They insist the gospel is but the message. One wonders, however, if they have read these verses closely enough:

> Now I would remind you, brothers, of the gospel I preached to you, which you received, in which you stand, and by which you are being saved, if you hold fast to the word I preached to you – unless you believed in vain. For I delivered to you as of first importance what I also received: that Christ died for our sins in accordance with the Scriptures, that he was buried, that he was raised on the third day in accordance with the Scriptures, and that he appeared to Cephas, then to the twelve (1 Corinthians 15:1-5).

Paul described his gospel as "preached" and "received." The good news message required faith, taking a stand against opposition and holding on to what was preached. One who failed to do these believed in vain. Does this sound like a message needing no response?

In Acts 8, Philip joined the chariot of the eunuch and began a discussion of Isaiah 53:7-8. The eunuch asked Philip, "About whom, I ask you, does the prophet say this, about himself or about someone else?" (Acts 8:34). Then "beginning with this Scripture [Philip] preached Jesus to him" (v. 35 NASB). Philip preached (*eueggelisato*) Jesus to him. The word "preached" comes from the word that means to preach the gospel or to evangelize. Philip "gospelized" Jesus (Acts 8:35). We do not know all that Philip said, but we do know his message included baptism: "And as they were going along the road they came to some water, and the eunuch said, 'See, here is water! What prevents me from being baptized?' " (v. 36 ESV). Philip's gospel preaching included the necessary response of faith and baptism. Moreover, the Scriptures speak of obeying the gospel in Romans 10:16; 2 Thessalonians 1:8; and

1 Peter 4:17. In each context, obedience is necessary to salvation. The direst circumstances come to those who do not obey.

Interestingly, some feel quite satisfied to cut out what God deems necessary in order to satisfy their desire to "get along" with those who differ. Some seem ready to jettison the truth for whatever new study some experts put forth. However, the truth is still the truth. The truth is not less true if it offends someone. It is not less true if it disagrees with "scholars." The truth is not less true just because it is difficult to obey. The truth is not less true whether I agree with it or whether I understand it. The truth is not less wise than the wisest of men. The truth in God's Word is wise and true because God said it. We must trust the wisdom of God to prove itself rather than accommodate it to current popular thinking. If the true wisdom of God in the Word is perfect, then any change from perfection defiles and leads to destruction.

If there is but one gospel, there cannot be two authentic gospels pleasing to God. If there are two, at least one must be false. Those who embrace the false, defiled gospel cannot expect it to provide the same promise as the true gospel. Those who preach a perverted gospel are accursed because they have lied and offered false hope to those who hear. When the Pharisees added their oral Torah to the Law and judged people's righteousness on the basis of their synthetic Judaism, Jesus explained to His disciples, "Every plant that my heavenly Father has not planted will be rooted up. Let them alone; they are blind guides. And if the blind lead the blind, both will fall into a pit" (Matthew 15:13-14). Those who trust in a distorted gospel do so to their own peril.

To this view, some people object that we do not understand the nature of grace. They hold the mere fact that people are mistaken about some doctrine does not mean they are nevertheless outside the grace of God. For them, people are more important than the doctrine, and the heart is more important than the ritual. Jesus, however, said that the Pharisees were blind guides headed for the pit; and Paul said the one who perverts the gospel is anathema. Apparently the Lord God thinks doctrine matters. It is, after all, the Lord's teaching. He gave it for a reason, and it offends Him when men change it. Adulterating the Word of God by changing it, even in the slightest, fails to respect God as God. It treats what is holy as if it were common and subject to change.

The grace of God does not sanction lies; it does not turn a lie into the truth. It cannot turn a substitute for baptism into true obedience. It cannot treat an infant sprinkled despite the truth as if the infant were intentionally obeying the truth. It cannot turn a baptism that confesses a belief contrary to God's teaching and opposes the truth into the "one baptism" of the New Testament. The grace of God does not turn entertainment and enterprise into worship. The grace of God does not excuse self-made worship that goes beyond the teaching of Christ. God's grace works in harmony with His teaching, not despite it. We cannot design our own religion as we please and expect God's grace to work anyway. Proclaiming ourselves right with God through some self-designed plan is no more effective today than it was in the days of the Pharisees. One cannot blend the one true faith with one's own ideas and expect a synthetic Christianity to have the hope and promise of New Testament Christianity.

Questions

1. What do the reigns of Jotham and of Ahaz in Judah tell us about the consequences of accommodation with error?

2. Should we strive to be "middle of the road" where truth is concerned?

3. What does the conflict between Azariah and Uzziah in 2 Chronicles 26 teach us about compromise with unauthorized worship?

4. Can moving toward an accommodation with error ever be a movement closer to God?

CHAPTER 11

POPULAR Religion

When sin is let in as a beggar, it remains in as a tyrant. The
Arabs have a fable of a miller who one day was startled by a
camel's nose thrust in the window of the room where he was
sleeping. "It is very cold outside," said the camel, "I only want to
get my nose in." The nose was let in, then the neck, and finally
the whole body. Presently the miller began to be extremely
inconvenienced at the ungainly companion he had obtained
in a room certainly not big enough for both. "If you are inconvenienced, you may leave," said the camel. "As for myself, I
shall stay where I am." There are many such camels knocking
at the human heart. A single worldly custom becomes the nose
of the camel, and it is not long before the entire body follows.
The Christian then finds his heart occupied by a vice which a
little while before peeped in so meekly. – Charles Spurgeon[1]

The phrase "popular religion" refers to what is believed, embraced
or perpetuated by a wide range of people. The concept "popular"
means it is well-liked and appreciated by many or by most. Some regard
popularity as an evidence of credibility. They might ask, "How could

so many people be wrong?" For them, right and truth are determined by counting noses. The most prevalent view must surely be the most correct and the best view to embrace.

Following God or Following the Crowd

Whether a view is popular or unpopular does not determine its truthfulness. When the 10 spies returned from the Promised Land, their bad report was adopted by nearly all Israel, yet this majority view proved disastrous (Numbers 13:28-33; 14:26-30). In this case, the faith of Caleb and Joshua alone proved correct. The people are not always right. Because he listened to the people, King Saul failed to obey the command of the Lord to "strike Amalek and utterly destroy" all he had (1 Samuel 15:3 NASB). When Saul brought back Agag and the best of the spoil, Samuel rebuked him for his disobedience (vv. 13-26). Listening to the people proved tragic; the Lord tore the kingdom of Israel from Saul that day (v. 28). Majorities do not change God; "the Glory of Israel will not lie or change His mind; for He is not a man that He should change His mind" (v. 29).

Nevertheless, just because a few embrace a belief does not ensure the correctness of that view either. The minority view of Korah and the 250 men who followed him in his rebellion demonstrated no virtue or wisdom. Their rebellion led to the destruction of their families (Numbers 16:25-35). God made it clear Moses was His choice to lead Israel. Opinion polls will tell us what people think and believe, but they do not determine spiritual truth. The ballots cast in any election do not necessarily determine the best candidate; the will of the majority has often proven flawed and foolish.

The revealed faith of Christianity has never been subject to the vote of men. Although men have often voted their convictions about religious matters, they can no more change the will of God than they can by voting change the brightness of the sun. God is not a man that He should change His mind. His teaching is true whether people accept it or not. Paul wrote to Timothy, "The saying is trustworthy, for: If we have died with him, we will also live with him; if we endure, we will also reign with him; if we deny him, he also will deny us; if we are faithless, he remains faithful – for he cannot deny himself" (2 Timothy 2:11-13 ESV).

Furthermore, Christianity is not a democracy but a kingdom. Its King alone makes the laws of the kingdom. What group of humans is wiser, more compassionate or more benevolent than Jesus? It is absurd to think we know more than He knows about people and the culture. It is absurd to think we can veto His laws! It is absurd and arrogant beyond measure to imagine He would not speak until we approved His teaching. Is it not absurd to think the omniscient Creator of the universe is somehow subject to the whims of cultural change and popular think-ing? Men who think the Lord needs their counsel about how to live or exercise faith reveal an amazing arrogance. With awe Paul exclaimed:

> Oh, the depth of the riches and wisdom and knowledge of God! How unsearchable are his judgments and how inscrutable his ways! "For who has known the mind of the Lord, or who has been his counselor? Or who has given a gift to him that he might be repaid?" For from him and through him and to him are all things. To him be glory forever. Amen (Romans 11:33-36).

When men believe they are gifted to invent a new religion patterned after the popular values of a changed society, they deceive themselves. God did not need our counsel to create the universe, and He does not need our counsel to understand what man needs or how man should live in the 21st century.

The Problems With Popular Thinking

Popular religion arises out of popular thinking. John Maxwell, in a chapter titled "Question Popular Thinking," quotes Kevin Myers saying, "The problem with popular thinking is that it doesn't require you to think at all." Good thinking is hard work, and Maxwell observes many people try to live life the easy way. "They don't want to do the hard work of thinking or pay the price of success. It's easier to do what other people do and hope they thought it out." [2]

Popular thinking is too average to understand the value of good thinking,[3] and popular religion is too content with mediocrity to appreciate or study the Scriptures to find true Christianity (Acts 17:11).

Popular thinking is too inflexible to realize the impact of changed thinking, and popular religion is so set in its ways it cannot see the real truth that can set it free (John 8:31-32).

Popular thinking is too lazy to think intentionally, and popular religion is too lazy to seek God's way rather than its own feelings (Jeremiah 6:16).

Popular thinking is too small to see the wisdom of big-picture thinking, and popular religion is too small to see "the whole counsel of God" (Acts 20:27).

Popular thinking is too satisfied to unleash the potential of focused thinking, and popular religion is too satisfied with itself to focus on handling the Scriptures accurately (2 Timothy 2:15).

Popular thinking is too trendy to embrace the lessons of reflective thinking, and popular religion is too trendy with feelings to reflect on the words that bring eternal life (John 6:66-70).

Popular thinking is too shallow to question whether it is credible, and popular religion is too shallow to question whether it should be accepted. It often deceives the multitudes with human philosophies that never measure up to the doctrine of Christ (Colossians 2:6-8).

Popular thinking is too proud to encourage the participation of shared thinking, and popular religion is too proud to be the instruction of the Lord. Such people wish to hear no more of the Holy One of Israel; they prefer pleasant words and illusions (Isaiah 30:8-11).

Popular thinking is too self-absorbed to experience the satisfaction of unselfish thinking, and popular religion is too self-absorbed in feelings and intuition to experience the satisfaction of obedience to God (Hebrews 5:8-9).

Popular thinking is too uncommitted to enjoy the return of bottom-line thinking, and popular religion is too uncommitted to Christ to enjoy the rewards of eternity (2 Timothy 4:6-8).

That which is popular can easily blind us to the truth. We can easily follow the crowd down an easy path without any thought to where it might lead. Many think if they see a lot of people doing something, then it must be good and right to do. People may think safety is in numbers, but that is not always true.

Coach Ed Skelton taught physical education in my eighth-grade junior high school. Our classes were in the Shawnee Municipal Auditorium that also served as a gym and was located just west of the main junior high building. Our class met third hour, just before lunch. One day the coach was away just as class was about to finish and the bell to ring for lunch. The class figured because the coach was away they could leave a couple of minutes early for lunch at the cafeteria or the brand new fast-food place across the street. All the boys left early but two of us, who waited until the bell rang.

The next day Coach Skelton had every boy who left early to come out to the line on the gym floor. Only two of us sat in the bleachers. He informed the class that the early exodus from the gym was reported by several teachers and the principal, who had seen the students through the windows. You could see red faces everywhere. To eighth graders, Coach Skelton seemed like a giant. He had only one punishment. His paddle was long and thick and hard. No one wanted to cross him, but almost everyone in the class had. Their only hope was in being in the majority. Maybe he wouldn't swing his paddle on so many. Each boy bent over, however, and the "board of education" sounded on every offender. Coach Skelton isn't God, but I learned that day that wrong is wrong even if nearly everyone does it. The belief of safety in numbers is a myth.

Popular religion loves the moment. It puts its confidence into the moment and will hardly let go. It resists the change that will return it to God, whose way is for all people in all places for all time. Many have gotten used to instrumental music, faith only and an entertainment style of religion. They do not realize their own unwillingness to see the truth. It is easier for them to label New Testament Christianity as "legalistic," "mean-spirited," "traditionalist" or "arrogant" than it is to seek the truth. If one calls names, one can dismiss another and not have to think or study.

God's Will Is Nonnegotiable

Acting on our own wisdom, our own judgment, rather than obeying God is always foolish. Solomon said in Proverbs 3:5-7, "Trust in the LORD with all your heart, and do not lean on your own understanding. In all your ways acknowledge him, and he will make straight your paths. Be not wise in your own eyes; fear the LORD, and turn away from evil." We must believe in God's wisdom, not our own. God sees and knows things we cannot see and know. His understanding is unlimited; we need to trust that what He teaches is right. Even when we do not understand why He says what He says, we need to trust His wisdom.

When considering what we believe and practice as Christians, let's ask, "Is this man's will or God's?" By that, I mean, can we read about this belief or practice in the New Testament? Or is this a belief or practice that came in later centuries by the design of men? If we can read that the Lord or the apostles taught this belief or practiced it, we can have confidence that God approves. But if it is something that began much later and is a departure from the truth, it should have no place in the life of a faithful Christian. We should leave the human theology and return to the Lord's will.

What God says matters. Jesus said, "The one who rejects me and does not receive my words has a judge; the word that I have spoken will judge him on the last day" (John 12:48). We cannot pick and choose what we like about God's teaching and what we do not like. The standard that will judge us on the last day is God's Word. God is sovereign, and He does not take opinion polls to determine the truth. Our society stresses political correctness, but God is not subject to our culture. Although we see changing opinions in our culture, God has spoken to all people in all places for all time (Jude 3). His will does not change.

Rather than thinking we can say and do religiously as we please, we should seek God's face and follow His will. The real issue is: Are we willing to yield our will to God's will and make Him Lord of our lives? Are we willing to listen to God? Many people seem to think they can live and believe as they wish. God won't know or care! But God does know and God does care. We cannot believe man-made doctrines and practice man-made traditions and expect God to be pleased. He wants us to follow His will and to give glory to His name. You cannot serve God and yourself!

Jesus said in Matthew 7:13-14, "Enter by the narrow gate. For the gate is wide and the way is easy that leads to destruction, and those who enter by it are many. For the gate is narrow and the way is hard that leads to life, and those who find it are few." These verses surprise most people. They think everyone is on the heavenly road, but that is not the way things really are. They think God is too gracious for the majority of people to be lost, but they have not listened to this verse. Matthew Henry comments on the broad way:

First, "You will have abundance of liberty in that way; the gate is wide, and stands wide open to tempt those that go right on their way. You may go in at this gate with all your lusts about you; it gives no check to your appetites, to your passions: you may walk in the way of your heart, and in the sight of your eyes; that gives room enough." It is a broad way, for there is nothing to hedge in those that walk in it, but they wander endlessly; a broad way, for there are many paths in it; there is choice of sinful ways, contrary to each other, but all paths in this broad way. Secondly, "You will have abundance of company in that way: many there be that go in at this gate, and walk in this way." If we follow the multitude, it will be to do evil: if we go with the crowd, it will be the wrong way. It is natural for us to incline to go down the stream, and do as the most do; but it is too great a compliment, to be willing to be damned for company, and to go to hell with them, because they will not go to heaven with us: if many perish, we should be the more cautious.[4]

The broad way is easy and filled with people. It is going to be popular, but the end is tragic. Not many people are willing to study for themselves and find the truth by looking into the words of Jesus. Many are willing to accept popular but unfaithful beliefs and practices.

Acting on popular wisdom or popular judgment rather than obeying God is always foolish. Solomon said in Proverbs 16:1-3, "The plans of the heart belong to man, but the answer of the tongue is from the LORD. All the ways of a man are pure in his own eyes, but the LORD weighs the spirit. Commit your work to the LORD, and your plans will be established." We must believe in God's wisdom, not our own. God sees and knows things we cannot see and know. His understanding is unlimited; we need to trust that what He teaches is right. Even when we do not understand why He says what He says, we need to trust His wisdom.

Asking the Right Questions

People should investigate their beliefs and practices, asking the question, "Is this biblical or is this something from men?" This would mean we would have to do some deeper study into the Bible to see what we would find. If we find a belief or practice is biblically approved, let's stay with it; but if it departs from the New Testament, we should abandon it. Thirty-five years ago I was preaching in a country church in Oklahoma. I met a sweet, wonderful lady named Oleta. She had been sprinkled as an infant in her church. When she became an adult, she got acquainted with some members of the church of Christ, and they began talking about the Bible.

When some of the members of the church told her that we baptize by immersion and only people old enough to believe and repent, she questioned that. The members replied, "Well, that's the way they did it in the Bible." This upset Oleta. She was just sure that what she had been taught was in the Bible. So she opened her Bible determined to justify her beliefs. She studied and studied, looking for verses to show the sprinkling of infants.

The more she read, however, the more she realized that what her friends had told her was right. The water baptism of the Bible was not sprinkling, and penitent faith always preceded baptism. Humbly, Oleta said, "I was studying to prove them wrong, and what I found was that Oleta was wrong." This honest lady saw that even cherished beliefs can be wrong. It was not easy for Oleta to come to that conclusion, but she was honest with God and with herself. She overcame popular beliefs to return to the teaching of Scripture.

Popular religion gives false hope. It is doubly dangerous because many are deceived into thinking that because it is both popular and religious, it must be spiritually approved. Millions cannot be wrong. But that is human thinking, human reasoning, and not divine wisdom. Judges 17 tells the story of Micah, who took 1,100 pieces of his mother's silver. When she found out that he possessed the silver, she rejoiced and took back her curse. And he restored the 1,100 pieces of silver to his mother. His mother said, "I dedicate the silver to the LORD from my hand for my son, to make a carved image and a metal image. Now therefore I will restore it to you" (v. 3). So when he restored the money to his mother, his mother took 200 pieces of silver and gave it to the silversmith, who made it into a carved image and a metal image. And it was in the house of Micah (vv. 3-4). Micah made a shrine and an ephod for his household gods. He appointed one of his sons as priest. The Scripture explains, "In those days there was no king in Israel. Everyone did what was right in his own eyes" (v. 6).

A young Levite from Bethlehem happened to go to the hill country of Ephraim, looking for a place to serve. Micah said to him, " 'Stay with me, and be to me a father and a priest, and I will give you ten pieces of silver a year and a suit of clothes and your living.' And the Levite went in. And the Levite was content to dwell with the man, and the young man became to him like one of his sons. And Micah ordained the Levite, and the young man became his priest, and was in the house of Micah. Then Micah said, 'Now I know that the LORD will prosper me, because I have a Levite as priest' " (Judges 17:10-13).

Micah's statement is amazing! One wonders how he could think the presence of a Levite as priest would make up for his presumptuous idol and shrine! It is as if by doing one thing right, he believed he could sanctify all the others. Having a priest, however, did not make up for his household gods. Yet what Micah did is no more amazing than people today who think they can invent a new church or blend Christianity with other religions. Self-made religion is a fantasy, even if it is popular and even if it has a shrine and a priest.

The emerging self-made religion has little more to commend it than Micah's shrine. If it is contrived from imagination and dreams, built upon the popular thinking of the day, it will give only lip service to the will of God. Calling a contrived religious gathering a church does not make it the church Jesus built any more than Aaron's golden calf was Jehovah (Exodus 32:1-6).

Popular religion is not willing to deal with controversy or conflict. It is willing to appease others by backing off on basic beliefs. For popular religionists, Jesus is not the only way to heaven. They may believe He is, but they are unwilling to take a stand on it. Because there is too much baggage with the word "inerrancy," popular religionists will not take a stand on whether the Word of God is utterly trustworthy.

For popular religionists, it is better to clam up and not take an "official" position on baptism than it is to stress what God has said about it. They will apologize for brethren who teach the truth on baptism rather than confront someone living with the false hope of a perverted baptism. Popular religionists put unity with people who are not brethren above pleasing God by obeying the truth. They would rather sanctify the false religionists than tell them to do what God wills.

Popular religion is more willing to dismiss what they discern as "divisive" than they are to continue in the words of Christ. They readily ignore doctrine, sin, guilt and judgment in their preaching and teaching, lest they offend or drive someone away from attending. They are people pleasers, taking into consideration the doctrine of truth will certainly turn people off. Reasoning from an overreaching view of grace, they assume they may set aside the authority of the truth. Those who hold this view of grace think they are magnifying it, but in truth they make it cheap by presuming upon it. They forget the truth is what teaches them about that grace. To be consistent, they cannot believe grace with any conviction from the evidence of the New Testament without accepting the other things the New Testament teaches. The Lord of grace is also the authoritative and holy Lord of truth.

Some preachers among churches of Christ have adopted an overreaching belief about grace. They believe grace so looks at the heart that one may ignore the ritual and with it the need for careful obedience to the will of God. This understanding of grace reminds one of a one-player team or a one-part quartet. As important as the pitcher is to a baseball team, he does not play alone. It takes all nine players. A quartet is not a quartet if only an alto sings; it takes all four voices. The new covenant of the Lord is filled with the marvelous and abundant grace of God, but that covenant of grace contains conditions and commandments. The narrow path of grace is also an obedient path to God. To call Jesus "Lord, Lord" requires obedience to the will of the Father in heaven (Matthew 7:21).

Popular religion is full of the broad and easy path that leads to destruction because it strives to find a way around the necessity of obedience. It is unwilling to pass through the narrow gate or walk the narrow way. It has no cross to bear. It has foolishly built its house on sand and looks as prosperous as the house built upon the rock. With false hope it promises security with God on presumed grace. Its house on sand comes from the fact it does not do the words of Christ it hears. Popular religion thinks God's grace allows it to pursue its own way, but nothing could be farther from the truth. Popular religion is the wide path and the house on sand (Matthew 7:13, 26-27); it is set on a course of destruction.

Questions

1. In 1 Samuel 15 we read of King Saul listening to the voice of the people. What was the outcome of this approach?

2. Why is the "broad way," with many fellow travelers, the way that leads to destruction?

3. How should one assess proposed changes in the work and worship of the church?

4. Is every person's opinion of equal value?

CHAPTER 12

WHO IS
My Brother?

Brotherhood must have a religious basis if it is to have any real significance. Without faith in the fatherhood of God, as Jesus and the prophets preached it, people have a pretty hard time being brotherly. They drift off into hate societies, or more often, into the society of the indifferent. – Edwin T. Dahlberg

P ostmodern people often say, "Whoever loves Jesus is my brother or sister." This statement first sounds compassionate and non-judgmental. One appreciates the sentiment behind such a statement, but claims such as this often ignore what God has to say. God is the progenitor of all His spiritual children. One cannot force his way into the family of God; only God has the right to decide who is and is not His child. People who share the same father or mother are considered family whether they acknowledge one another or not. Common parent-age defines and qualifies the relationship of siblings. [1]

From the beginning, however, common parentage does not guarantee closeness of heart. Brothers of the flesh are often not brothers in heart. Cain out of sin and jealousy killed his brother Abel (Genesis 4:8; 1 John 3:12). Jacob feared Esau after he swindled Esau out of his birthright

(Genesis 32:11). The brothers of Joseph out of hatred and jealousy sold their brother into slavery in Egypt and told their father he had been killed by a beast (37:23-33). Absalom hated and killed his brother Amnon for violating their sister Tamar (2 Samuel 13). Shamefully, many people despise their siblings. Solomon rightly remarked in Proverbs 17:17, "A friend loves at all times, and a brother is born for adversity."

In a spiritual sense, some of the same problems of jealousy and hatred arise between brethren. Paul warned brethren in the churches of Galatia:

> For you were called to freedom, brothers. Only do not use your freedom as an opportunity for the flesh, but through love serve one another. For the whole law is fulfilled in one word: "You shall love your neighbor as yourself." But if you bite and devour one another, watch out that you are not consumed by one another (Galatians 5:13-15).

Unfortunately, many brethren do bite and devour one another out of jealousy to gain some advantage. Paul speaks of some who preach out of "rivalry, not sincerely but thinking to afflict me in my imprisonment" (Philippians 1:17). Such people often do not know who their brethren are or how to treat them. It is easy to see, then, why the question, "Who is my brother?" is so significant.

If I am a child of God and another person is a child of God, then we are brethren. This should be easy to understand and accept, but many deceivers are in the world. Jesus warned of wolves in sheep's clothing (Matthew 7:15), and Paul suffered from false brethren (2 Corinthians 11:26; Galatians 2:4). John therefore urged us, "Beloved, do not believe every spirit, but test the spirits to see whether they are from God, for many false prophets have gone out into the world" (1 John 4:1). Testing to see who is in Christ is not sinful. Asking "Who is my brother?" helps us to avoid what is false and to remain in what is right. Truth settles our identity in Christ; one is sanctified by the truth (John 17:17). One is born again by obedience to the truth (1 Peter 1:22). One is a true disciple by abiding in the words of Jesus, and the truth sets him free (John 8:31-32). Therefore we must turn to the truth to learn who is truly a child of God and a brother in the Lord.

Who Is My Brother?

Jesus Christ has a right to decide who is and is not a Christian brother; and no human can change His will. What men think or believe is irrelevant. Our task is to ask what Jesus has said. Our focus is not to decide who is right but to settle what is right. Nor is it our purpose to be sectarian. Our goal is to go to heaven and to lead others there based on the only accurate guide we have – the Bible. So, we are asking the Bible for God's answers to this important question: "Who is a Christian?"

Many people today are "nominal" Christians; that is, they are Christians in name only. They call themselves Christians but do not live the life of a Christian, do not go to church, seldom pray, and rarely read their Bible. Many who call themselves Christians have never considered what God commands them to do to respond to His grace in Christ.

A Christian is one who belongs to Christ, who is His disciple and a church member, who willingly follows the Lord at any cost, who loves the Lord and trusts in Him, and who lives a life that glorifies Jesus. A Christian has taken up his cross daily and wears the yoke of Christ. A Christian is one who has purified his life because he has fixed his hope on the second coming of Christ. A Christian is one who loves others the way Jesus loves them, who sacrifices freely for the blessing of others. A Christian is one who feels a spiritual duty to share the good news of salvation with others. Discipleship means I am willing to follow the Lord and do His will. Many people want the blessings of Christianity, but true disciples do His will. They do not play Christianity; they live it, talk it, walk it, love it and share it.

Are there people who think they are Christians but have no relationship with the Lord? The Lord said in Matthew 7:21, "Not everyone who says to me, 'Lord, Lord,' will enter the kingdom of heaven, but the one who does the will of my Father who is in heaven." Thinking I have a relationship with the Lord and having a saving relationship with the Lord are two different things. Wishing and claiming I am a citizen of the United Kingdom of Great Britain does not make me one. I must follow the laws of that nation to become a citizen. I cannot edit or set aside their laws, proclaim myself a citizen, and expect to vote in their next election. I would have no credentials unless they issued them. Nor can we have citizenship in the kingdom of heaven without the express approval of God.

One could never be considered an approved brother in the Lord apart from faith. Without faith it is impossible to please God (Hebrews 11:6). The person who disbelieves is condemned and judged already (Mark 16:16; John 3:18). In John 8:24, Jesus said, "I told you that you would die in your sins; for unless you believe that I am he, you will die in your sins." Unless a person believes Jesus is the Christ, the Messiah, he is still in sin and cannot please God.

Faith is essential to one's becoming a child of God. John said of Jesus, "He came to his own, and his own people did not receive him. But to all who did receive him, who believed in his name, he gave the right to become children of God, who were born, not of blood nor of the will of the flesh nor of the will of man, but of God" (John 1:11-13). Not everyone who believes has become a child of God, but faith in Jesus Christ opens the way for one to become a child of God. Philip would not baptize the eunuch until he came to faith (Acts 8:36-37), and there is no need to baptize someone today who does not believe.

As I noted in Chapter 8, a preacher in the church of Christ recently proclaimed that he told a woman who was sprinkled as an infant in a denomination that she was saved, was a sister in Christ, and was going to heaven.[2] With supposedly great compassion, the preacher reassured her that she was right before God. In the same breath, he apologized that members of the church of Christ had possibly judged her. How can baptism before the time of faith make anyone a child of God? One has no right to give another false hope in suggesting that an alternate plan of obeying the gospel prior to faith will yield the same result as obeying the truth.

Peter said, "Having purified your souls by your obedience to the truth for a sincere brotherly love, love one another earnestly from a pure heart, since you have been born again, not of perishable seed but of imperishable, through the living and abiding word of God" (1 Peter 1:22-23). A person who is too young to believe is also too young to know he has obeyed the truth. Those who give false hope to others do them no favors but rather great harm that can cost them their souls. One can be born again into Christ only when he or she has obeyed the truth of the gospel.

Because no denominations are ever contemplated in Scripture and the division that is caused by them is clearly condemned (1 Corinthians

1:10-13; Galatians 5:19-21), we cannot regard members of denomina-tions as New Testament Christians. Because the Lord and His teach-ing are the only standards by which we can settle who is and is not a Christian brother, we should not speak more broadly than Scripture to account people as believers who are not considered believers by God.

Jesus also said in Luke 13:3 and 5, "No, I tell you; but unless you repent, you will all likewise perish." No person can be right with God and counted a brother in Christ Jesus who is unwilling to forsake his sins. Repentance is necessary!

Being a Christian is not a private matter. The Lord asks us to con-fess him before others. Jesus said, "So everyone who acknowledges me before men, I also will acknowledge before my Father who is in heaven, but whoever denies me before men, I also will deny before my Father who is in heaven" (Matthew 10:32-33).

All Children of God Are "Born Again"

Jesus also said in John 3:3, "Truly, truly, I say to you, unless one is born again he cannot see the kingdom of God." If one is a Christian at all, he is born again. Being born again means one is transformed by God into a new creature. Paul said, "Therefore, if anyone is in Christ, he is a new creation. The old has passed away; behold, the new has come" (2 Corinthians 5:17). "Nicodemus said to Him, 'How can a man be born when he is old? Can he enter a second time into his mother's womb and be born?' Jesus answered, 'Truly, truly, I say to you, unless one is born of water and the Spirit, he cannot enter into the kingdom of God' " (John 3:4-5). The new birth Jesus mentioned is comprised of water and the Spirit. The early church fathers understood this to be baptism, and they are right. This new birth takes place when a person is baptized (immersed) into Christ for the forgiveness of sins.

The Lord said in Mark 16:16, "Whoever believes and is baptized will be saved, but whoever does not believe will be condemned." It is obvious that an unbeliever has no reason to be baptized. However, if we want to be saved, we will believe and will be baptized into Christ. At that time we become a new creature and enter the kingdom of God, the church. The New Testament never contemplates a Christian who is not baptized. In Acts 2:38, Peter told the people to repent and be baptized in the name of Jesus Christ for the forgiveness of their sins. Ananias told Saul of Tarsus, "And now why do you wait? Rise and be baptized and wash away your sins, calling on his name" (Acts 22:16). Baptism (immersion in water) is that time when the old man of sin dies and we rise to "walk in newness of life" (Romans 6:4). It is the turning point between the sinner and the saint. We die with Christ to the old man and are raised up by God to walk a new life as God forgives our sins and causes us to be born again. We are baptized into the death of Christ and come into contact with the blood of Jesus that cleanses us from all sin. We are baptized into Christ and put Him on (Galatians 3:26-27). The Bible never contemplates an unbaptized brother any more than it contemplates an atheist brother.

Brotherhood and Fellowship Are Not the Same

Merely because one is a brother does not necessarily mean that he remains in fellowship with the Lord or the church. Just because one believes does not ensure that he will keep on believing. Psalm 106 tells the story of the children of Israel in the wilderness. In verse 12, "they believed His words"; but they quickly forgot His works (v. 13) and in time did not believe in His word (v. 24). Their loss of faith did not mean they stopped being brothers; it did mean they fell out of God's grace and favor. Commenting on the failure of Israel in the wilderness, the writer of Hebrews speaks directly to Christians in Hebrews 3:12-13: "Take care, brothers, lest there be in any of you an evil, unbelieving heart, leading you to fall away from the living God. But exhort one another every day, as long as it is called 'today,' that none of you may be hardened by the deceitfulness of sin." Brothers can fall away from the living God and lose His loving favor.

In 1 Corinthians 5, a brother was committing great sin by living with his father's wife. The Corinthian brethren were arrogant in allowing this to happen rather than mourning over his sin. Paul took immediate action against this brother by delivering "this man to Satan for the destruction of the flesh, so that his spirit may be saved in the day of the Lord" (1 Corinthians 5:5). Paul described the implications of this act of "disfellowshiping":

> But now I am writing to you not to associate with anyone who bears the name of brother if he is guilty of sexual immorality or greed, or is an idolater, reviler, drunkard, or swindler – not even to eat with such a one. For what have I to do with judging outsiders? Is it not those inside the church whom you are to judge? God judges those outside. "Purge the evil person from among you" (1 Corinthians 5:11-13).

It is clear from this passage that one can be a brother but out of fellowship with God and with other brethren.

Some brethren in Thessalonica were acting in an undisciplined manner by failing to work and by becoming busybodies. Paul instructed the Thessalonians to "keep away from any brother who is walking in idleness and not in accord with the tradition that you received from us" (2 Thessalonians 3:6). Paul demanded that these undisciplined brothers go back to work in a quiet fashion and to eat their own bread. He added, "If anyone does not obey what we say in this letter, take note of that person, and have nothing to do with him, that he may be ashamed. Do not regard him as an enemy, but warn him as a brother" (vv. 14-15). Brethren who are out of fellowship with the church need to be treated kindly as brothers. Kindness in this instance, however, means an admonition, i.e., a warning that expects change.

Further, brethren out of envy or deception can get caught up in efforts that destroy the truth and divide the church. Paul instructed Titus in how to deal with a person who is teaching factious doctrines: "But avoid foolish controversies, genealogies, dissensions, and quarrels about the law, for they are unprofitable and worthless. As for a person who stirs up division, after warning him once and then twice, have nothing more to do with him, knowing that such a person is warped and sinful; he is self-condemned" (Titus 3:9-11). Faithful Christians cannot have fellowship with those who bind human opinions or false doctrines that split the church. When leaders can no longer see change in a factious brother through admonition, they are left with no other choice than to disfellowship him. A man is not factious because he disagrees over some point of Scripture; he is factious when he presses or binds his opinion or view to the point that he disrupts the unity of the congregation. Leaders cannot permit the unity of the church to be disrupted by false doctrine or human opinions.

Paul warned the elders of the church at Ephesus to be on their guard because "fierce ["savage," NASB] wolves will come in among you, not sparing the flock; and from among your own selves will arise men speaking twisted things, to draw away the disciples after them" (Acts 20:29-30). Sometimes the greatest threat comes not from the outside but from brethren inside the church. Elders must:

> … hold firm to the trustworthy word as taught, so that [they] may be able to give instruction in sound doctrine and also to rebuke those who contradict it. For there are many who are insubordinate, empty talkers and deceivers, especially those of the circumcision party. They must be silenced, since they are upsetting whole families by teaching for shameful gain what they ought not to teach (Titus 1:9-11).

Elders (and preachers) must stand as guardians of the church against the false doctrines of men. They must do so even when that false doctrine arises from a brother they love (cf. Deuteronomy 13).

God expects His people to hold so closely to the truth that they will not give support to a false teacher. God regards false teaching as evil; those who support false teachers participate in that evil. John wrote:

> Everyone who goes on ahead and does not abide in the teaching of Christ, does not have God. Whoever abides in the teaching has both the Father and the Son. If anyone comes to you and does not bring this teaching, do not receive him into your house or give him any greeting, for whoever greets him takes part in his wicked works (2 John 9-11).

Although some brethren restrict applying this passage to false teaching regarding the divine-human nature of Jesus Christ, by implication the principle can apply far more broadly. The sin of 2 John 9 is in going beyond the teaching of the Lord. If it is sinful to do so about the nature of Jesus, is it not also sinful, by implication, to go beyond anything the Lord teaches? It is evil to add to the Word of God, and true disciples, true brethren, remain in the Word of the Lord (John 8:31).

Truth makes men right with God and right as brothers. When any brother strays from the truth, love demands that he be warned and perhaps disciplined. He does not cease to be a brother because of his errors, but no one can continue in error and sin and remain in the grace and favor of God. Whether he is a brother we love or one we do not know, we cannot fellowship or tolerate moral or doctrinal error. James said, "My brothers, if anyone among you wanders from the truth and someone brings him back, let him know that whoever brings back a sinner from his wandering will save his soul from death and will cover a multitude of sins" (James 5:19-20). May we always be loving yet act honorably with our brethren.

The Great Communion

The Disciples of Christ Historical Society called for a "Great Communion" on Oct. 4, 2009 to commemorate the bicentennial of Thomas Campbell's *Declaration and Address*. They said, "While there are other events and documents that we have also remembered, everyone agreed that this 1809 document truly formed the constitution for our [Stone-Campbell] movement." The task force for this event wanted to stress the unity that Thomas Campbell called for in 1809. This, they thought, "was the perfect opportunity to remember Thomas Campbell and his contribution, as well as live out the unity that we all hold so dear." [3]

They hoped "that congregations of all three streams will gather in communities all across the globe on that special Sunday and share communion together." They thought to join the Disciples of Christ, the Independent Christian Church, and the churches of Christ in a communion service so they might find unity. "Our prayer is that on this one day, with communion being shared by Stone-Campbell believers all around the world, that a true beginning will be found to complete Christ's desire for all humanity: May they all be one." In his *Declaration and Address*, Campbell said, "Ye desire union in Christ with all them that love him; so do we."

This call for unity asked the churches of Christ (supposedly of the American Restoration Movement) to set aside their convictions on many serious biblical issues and grant fellowship to some in error and some who are not Christians at all (according to Scripture). Loving the Lord is an essential characteristic of Christianity, but loving the Lord is not the only qualification of Christianity. Those behind the Great Communion seek to unify the estranged without dealing with the reasons for that estrangement.

Churches of Christ more than a century ago came to be estranged from the Disciples of Christ and the Independent Christian Churches/churches of Christ over the use of instrumental music in Christian worship and the missionary societies. The Christian Churches/churches of Christ pulled away more recently from the Disciples of Christ over open fellowship (the sprinkling of infants for baptism) and the abusive control of the denominational structure.[4] For churches of Christ, the refusal to use instruments in worship and the denial of sprinkling infants for baptism are not just opinions. Basing their beliefs on God's Holy Word, churches of Christ regard human innovations such as instrumental music and sprinkling infants as sinful practices. The Disciples of Christ point to Thomas and Alexander Campbell as their leaders, but they have far removed themselves from the beliefs and practices of the Campbells.

To fellowship the Disciples of Christ, churches of Christ would have to set aside the Word of God for a human tradition (Matthew 15:8-13), violate their consciences (Romans 14:23), and recognize as brethren those who have never scripturally come to Christ. Surely such an action is an offense against God. To fellowship and support those who teach and practice false doctrines means that one shares in their evil deeds (2 John 10-11). When someone practices sin, Christians should mourn, not celebrate (1 Corinthians 5:1-2). When those who speak and act contrary to the apostolic doctrine continue in their practices, faithful Christians must warn, mark and withdraw from them (Romans 16:17-18; Titus 3:10-11).

Those who set aside their faith and violate their consciences to support those in error break their fellowship with God. Unity with others holds little value to the person who loses his relationship with the Father and the Son. The Scripture says:

> And by this we know that we have come to know him, if
> we keep his commandments. Whoever says "I know him"

but does not keep his commandments is a liar, and the truth is not in him, but whoever keeps his word, in him truly the love of God is perfected. By this we may know that we are in him: whoever says he abides in him ought to walk in the same way in which he walked (1 John 2:3-6).

No doubt the churches of Christ wish and pray to have unity with those from whom they have been estranged, but unity can come only when all parties hold to the same standard of truth and turn away from error. Before Jesus prayed for unity, He first set apart His disciples in the truth (John 17:17). Jesus understood the Word the Father gave to Him was the truth. Blending God's people who hold to God's truth to a body who say human innovations are permissible leads to corruption. To claim we know God while holding to sinful human innovations is to lie; this is not the truth. The corrupted become more unified, but this does not glorify God. Glorifying God means the corrupted must repent and leave their error and once again obey His commandments. Those who are not yet obedient to the gospel, however much they say they love God, must obey the Lord's teaching about baptism.

One cannot reach the unity for which Christ prayed by following misplaced sentiments and ditching the truth. Our identity as true disciples arises from remaining in the words of Christ (John 8:31-32), and only the truth can set us free. Men have no right to "one-up" God. The human suggestion of a "great communion" shows utter disrespect for God's instructions for the Lord's Supper. Are human suggestions greater than God's instructions? The communion the Lord founded is already kept in the Lord's church worldwide each first day of the week. The notion we can set a particular Lord's day above others presumes too much.

The Bible gives no place for setting a man beside the Lord in a memorial meal. Thomas Campbell, although having many fine qualities, did not die for the church. His blood could not in any way forgive sin. Where is there any biblical instruction or precedent for remembering a human being with Jesus in the Lord's Supper?

When men ditch their Biblical authority for cultural and historical significance, they reveal a mindset little different from the pagan who exalted idols. Let us be content with the instructions of the New Testament; then we will not corrupt the truth. The way to unity arises from a commitment to the truth of God by which we are sanctified. Without this sanctification in the truth, all talk of true discipleship and fellowship is fruitless. Those who left the truth for human innovations must come back to the truth to find unity with the Lord and His people. They must put away their sinful practices if they wish to unite to the Lord. When they unite with the Lord, then they can find unity with His people.

Although the Disciples of Christ Historical Society may regard churches of Christ as part of the American Restoration Movement, we are more concerned with what the Lord thinks and desires for us. I was not baptized into the name of the Restoration Movement; I was baptized into Christ. I did not come to Jesus Christ to join an American movement; I took up my cross to follow the Lord Himself. I embraced the ideals of the Restoration Plea not to become a member of the Restoration Movement but to become a member of the Lord's body. Although I agree with much of Campbell's *Declaration and Address*, I am bound under and only to the "law of Christ" (1 Corinthians 9:21).

Questions

1. When members of our physical family leave the faith, we have a strong desire to compromise our convictions so that they will be all right where they are. How can we avoid this temptation to sacrifice truth because of sentiment?

2. What distinguishes appropriate from inappropriate association with various denominations?

3. If a denominational group operates a benevolence program, should members of the church participate as workers in it?

4. Are there Christians in various denominational groups? Are there unimmersed Christians?

CHAPTER 13

BACK TO the Cross

I have been crucified with Christ. It is no longer I who live, but Christ who lives in me. And the life I now live in the flesh I live by faith in the Son of God, who loved me and gave himself for me (Galatians 2:20).

And he said to all, "If anyone would come after me, let him deny himself and take up his cross daily and follow me. For whoever would save his life will lose it, but whoever loses his life for my sake will save it" (Luke 9:23-24).

If then you have been raised with Christ, seek the things that are above, where Christ is, seated at the right hand of God. Set your minds on things that are above, not on things that are on earth. For you have died, and your life is hidden with Christ in God. When Christ who is your life appears, then you also will appear with him in glory (Colossians 3:1-4).

Nothing is wrong with postmodern civilization that a long look at the cross of Christ would not solve. We must not doubt the power of the Word or the power of the love of Christ. Jesus said, "And I, when I am lifted up from the earth, will draw all people to myself"

(John 12:32). We must not suppose anything is equal to the power of the cross to draw, to convict and to convert. Those who reduce the place of the cross have little spiritually to suggest, little to believe, and little to hope for. The cross is God's undeniable demonstration of love and commitment to our eternal life.

Priorities Directed by the Cross

Paul said, "And I, when I came to you, brothers, did not come proclaiming to you the testimony of God with lofty speech or wisdom. For I decided to know nothing among you except Jesus Christ and him crucified" (1 Corinthians 2:1-2). Paul, the student of Gamaliel (Acts 22:3), was perhaps the most educated of the apostles and writers of the New Testament. He quoted freely from the poets Aratus (17:28) and Epimenides (Titus 1:12), showing his wide knowledge of Greek literature. A Jew by birth of the tribe of Benjamin, a Hebrew of Hebrews, a Pharisee by sect (Philippians 3:5), and a Roman citizen of the city of Tarsus, Paul enjoyed a multicultural life with many strong influences. There are good reasons to believe that if Paul were not a member of the Sanhedrin, he would likely have been elected after the death of Stephen.[1]

Paul, however, was willing to give it all up to be a Christian. Something more was vital to his heart than his pedigree and cultural prosperity.

> But whatever gain I had, I counted as loss for the sake of Christ. Indeed, I count everything as loss because of the surpassing worth of knowing Christ Jesus my Lord. For his sake I have suffered the loss of all things and count them as rubbish, in order that I may gain Christ and be found in him, not having a righteousness of my own that comes from the law, but that which comes through faith in Christ, the righteousness from God that depends on faith – that I may know him and the power of his resurrection, and may share his sufferings, becoming like him in his death, that by any means possible I may attain the resurrection from the dead (Philippians 3:7-11).

Paul wanted Christ more than his heritage as a Pharisee and a Hebrew of Hebrews. He wanted to have the fellowship of His sufferings. Paul was willing to take up his cross daily and follow Christ (Luke 9:23). He chose the righteousness of the cross over the righteousness of the Law. Although he was born to a prominent family, well versed in Judaism and Phariseeism, his choice was easy. The cross of Christ comes first; everything else is rubbish. Considering his rabbinic education and the advantages of his Pharisaical fraternity, this was a monumental sacrifice; but nothing comes close to knowing Christ. Compared with the resurrection, it doesn't even count!

The Cross Bridges Cultural Differences

Paul wanted Jesus Christ. He wanted to know Him. He wanted to be conformed to Him in His death, to share in His sufferings, and "to attain the resurrection" (Philippians 3:11). Paul had no desire to do as some of the others in his day, to remake Christianity in the image of Judaism, especially Pharisaical Judaism. He had no desire to remake Christianity over in the image of Greek philosophy or Roman jurisprudence. He stopped investing in his old life in Judaism so that he could build his new life in Christ.

> Not that I have already obtained this or am already perfect, but I press on to make it my own, because Christ Jesus has made me his own. Brothers, I do not consider that I have made it my own. But one thing I do: forgetting what lies behind and straining forward to what lies ahead, I press on toward the goal for the prize of the upward call of God in Christ Jesus (Philippians 3:12-14).

Paul did not allow his cultural heritage to have such a hold on his life that he lost sight of Christ and His cross. When a person takes up His cross, he must deny himself and forget the past. One will not die to himself if he is unwilling to deny himself.

Although Paul had much to boast about in his life, he looked not to his cultural heritage but to the cross. "But far be it from me to boast except in the cross of our Lord Jesus Christ, by which the world has been crucified to me, and I to the world" (Galatians 6:14). Indeed, the cross of Christ was the instrument by which Paul died to the world. Paul could not have Christ and allow the world to live in him. He chose Christ over the world, over the lust of the flesh, over the lust of the eyes, and over the pride of life.

The Cross Is a Point of Decision

The real rub of Christianity cries: Will I crucify myself to the world and allow the world to be crucified to me? Will I, having died to my own will, allow the will of Jesus to rule in my life completely? Will I leave the old man of sin behind so that I can conform to the image of Jesus Christ (Colossians 3:9-10)? Will I deny myself and lose my life for the sake of Christ, so that I may be saved eternally?

> So you also must consider yourselves dead to sin and alive to God in Christ Jesus. Let not sin therefore reign in your mortal body, to make you obey its passions. Do not present your members to sin as instruments for unrighteousness, but present yourselves to God as those who have been brought from death to life, and your members to God as instruments for righteousness (Romans 6:11-13).

I cannot edit Christianity to suit my own desires and say I have died to the world. I cannot reinvent my faith with a little of this and a little of that to suit what I think my culture wants me to believe and to practice. My culture did not bear a cross for my soul. My culture does not promise me anything as the Lord does. My culture cannot give me everlasting life.

Men designed the cross to bring about a slow and an agonizing death. A society that dotes on ease and entertainment, that demands religion accommodate the people, will not likely have the grit to bear a cross or die to self. The Lord, who bore a cross, said, "And whoever does not take his cross and follow me is not worthy of me" (Matthew 10:38). One must wonder how the religious playtime many churches aim for will lead anyone to the maturity where one will die for Christ.

The Cross Requires Personal Repentance

Many churches preach the cross of Christ; they want the salvation He provides. But they also preach a Christian faith without the cross each individual is to bear. They are all too ready to take their cues from polls and surveys rather than from the New Testament. Some church leaders feel so bullied to accommodate culture they have dismissed the personal cross Christians are called to bear. They imagine people are still worthy of Christ without taking up their cross to follow Him. They imagine Christ's heart is so big He won't reject anyone for anything. They take His grace for granted and cheapen it.

Must Jesus bear the cross alone, and all the world go free?
No, there's a cross for everyone, and there's a cross for me.

Many sing the old hymn, but they do not believe it.

Back to the Cross

We must return to New Testament Christianity, where taking up our cross means we have died to self, died to the world, and died to human deceptions and innovations. Taking up our cross means we follow Christ; we sanctify Him as Lord in our hearts (1 Peter 3:15). Being crucified with Christ means we live by faith in the Son of God, who loved us and gave Himself for us (Galatians 2:20). The cross radically changes our hearts and lives. "For the love of Christ controls us, because we have concluded this: that one has died for all, therefore all have died; and he died for all, that those who live might no longer live for themselves but for him who for their sake died and was raised" (2 Corinthians 5:14-15).

God so loved us He gave His Son on the cross to die for our sins (John 3:16; Romans 5:6-8). He invested the cleansing blood in our souls to transform our lives and make new people out of us. In baptism we rise to walk in newness of life (6:4); the old man of sin is crucified and dead. God never intended for us to remain where we were. He saved, cleansed, regenerated and renewed us to make us into a new kind of people, conformed to His image. Paul explained the mind of God in Titus 2:11-14:

> For the grace of God has appeared, bringing salvation for all people, training us to renounce ungodliness and worldly passions, and to live self-controlled, upright, and godly lives in the present age, waiting for our blessed hope, the appearing of the glory of our great God and Savior Jesus Christ, who gave himself for us to redeem us from all lawlessness

and to purify for himself a people for his own possession who are zealous for good works.

God invested the blood of Christ in you and me to redeem, purify and reshape us. God wanted us to put away sin so we could live righteously and zealously for what is good. The cross motivates people to live godly; a godly person takes God seriously in every aspect of life. He lives a morally pure life because God matters. He treats others fairly and kindly because God matters. He forgives others because God forgave him. He holds to the truth of the Bible because it is God's truth. The mindset of a godly person dictates how he lives his life; he can no longer shrink back in neutrality or passivity about important issues. He will sacrifice his own will for the will of God. He will change his heart and behavior because his heart belongs to God. He has lost his life for the sake of the Lord (Luke 9:24).

The Cross Motivates Our Outreach

The cross of Christ turns the heart of the disciples "to seek and to save the lost" (Luke 19:10). Realizing our own redemption and salvation, we cannot but think of others whose souls are not yet covered by the blood of Jesus. Paul said, "From now on, therefore, we regard no one according to the flesh" (2 Corinthians 5:16). Because the eternal is on our hearts and minds, we do not look at people the way we used to see them. We know they have souls that will stand before God in the judgment, and we want them to enter the heavenly city. Taking up the cross of Christ puts one into the business of leading others to Christ. He pulls for anything that will lead people to Christ and to righteousness and against anything that keeps one from the Lord. He knows he is in a war for souls.

We too are in the spiritual war, and we cannot afford to lose. We do not fight for money or for power. We do not fight for democracy or for our physical lives. We fight for the everlasting welfare of our souls and the souls of those whom we may influence. If we fail, we suffer eternally; and we may lead others to lose their souls. Our battle is a personal one, and we cannot avoid the conflict.

In this battle we have the toughest of foes, one who is greatly experienced, cunning and skillful. We cannot take the devil for granted. He knows our weaknesses and understands the subtleties of deception. He will not fight fair and shows no mercy. But in all this, we do not despair: Jesus overcame Satan at the cross (Hebrews 2:14-15; 1 John 3:8). The Lord can also help us overcome. The Holy Spirit through Paul said:

> Finally, be strong in the Lord and in the strength of his might. Put on the whole armor of God, that you may be able to stand against the schemes of the devil. For we do not wrestle against flesh and blood, but against the rulers, against the authorities, against the cosmic powers over this present darkness, against the spiritual forces of evil in the heavenly places. Therefore take up the whole armor of God, that you may be able to withstand in the evil day, and having done all, to stand firm (Ephesians 6:10-13).

Indeed, the Lord has outfitted us with the full armor of God and has strengthened us with truth, righteousness, the gospel of peace, faith, salvation and the Word of God. More than that, He has given us the privilege of prayer (vv. 14-20). We can "withstand in the evil day," and having done everything, we can stand firm (v. 13). This brings us to a critical question.

How Did Jesus Bear the Cross?

How did Jesus remain on the cross? How did He endure the shame, the agonizing pain, the humiliation, and the slander? Why did He not call 12 legions of angels to destroy them all (Matthew 26:53)? The arrested Lord Jesus answered this question with a rhetorical question: "How then will the Scriptures be fulfilled, which say that it must happen this way?"

• **First, Jesus remained on the cross out of a sense of duty.** He obeyed His Father (Philippians 2:8), praying for the will of His Father to be done (Matthew 26:39, 42). "Although he was a son, he learned obedience through what he suffered. And being made perfect, he became the source of eternal salvation to all who obey him" (Hebrews 5:8-9).

We too must wholeheartedly embrace a sense of duty and devotion if we are to bear our own cross. Some see devotion and duty as slavery.

So be it. I am happily His slave. My Lord and Master bought me with His blood, and I am not my own any longer (1 Corinthians 6:19-20; 1 Peter 1:18-19). In a democratic republic with many freedoms, to speak of slavery seems alien. However, until we understand we belong to the Lord, we will be fighting God instead of fighting with Him. Jesus found peace and strength to face the cross by conquering His own will and submitting to His Father. When He emptied Himself and humbled Himself in obedience at Gethsemane, He was prepared for victory at Calvary.

• **Second, Jesus remained on the cross out of love and trust.** The Son wholeheartedly loved and trusted His Father. Although the shame of an unjust trial and a painful death hung heavily in His heart, Jesus found strength to endure through His relationship with His Father. On the night Jesus was betrayed, He understood fully what was to happen to Him. Speaking of His death and leaving the disciples, Jesus explained, "And now I have told you before it takes place, so that when it does take place you may believe. I will no longer talk much with you, for the ruler of this world is coming. He has no claim on me, but I do as the Father has commanded me, so that the world may know that I love the Father. Rise, let us go from here" (John 14:29-31). Jesus expressed His undeniable love for His Father through obedience to His will. He would do "exactly" what His Father wanted.

Love is the powerful motivator of Christianity. We are controlled by His love to live for Him (2 Corinthians 5:14-15). Our love arises from our knowledge of God and His love for us (1 John 4:9-11, 19). John expressed thanks for this love:

> See what kind of love the Father has given to us, that we should be called children of God; and so we are. The reason why the world does not know us is that it did not know him. Beloved, we are God's children now, and what we will be has not yet appeared; but we know that when he appears we shall be like him, because we shall see him as he is. And everyone who thus hopes in him purifies himself as he is pure (1 John 3:1-3).

Love motivates us to forsake the world and its lusts so that we may live for the Lord and glorify him (1 John 2:15-17).

Because the Son loved the Father, He knew He could entrust Himself to the Father's will and find the help He needed. Peter explained:

> For to this you have been called, because Christ also suffered for you, leaving you an example, so that you might follow in his steps. He committed no sin, neither was deceit found in his mouth. When he was reviled, he did not revile in return; when he suffered, he did not threaten, but continued entrusting himself to him who judges justly. He himself bore our sins in his body on the tree, that we might die to sin and live to righteousness. By his wounds you have been healed (1 Peter 2:21-24).

Not only did God help Jesus through His pain and humiliation on the cross, but He also can help us. Peter advised the Christians who would undergo persecution, "Therefore let those who suffer according to God's will entrust their souls to a faithful Creator while doing good" (1 Peter 4:19).

• **Third, Jesus endured the cross for the joy set before Him (Hebrews 12:2).** The writer of Hebrews advised the brethren of his day to remain faithful. He pointed to other saints (men of whom the world is not worthy) who remained faithful in times of great testing and gained approval by their faith and obedience (Hebrews 11). These spiritual giants testify to us of the victory that comes to the faithful:

> Therefore, since we are surrounded by so great a cloud of witnesses, let us also lay aside every weight, and sin which clings so closely, and let us run with endurance the race that is set before us, looking to Jesus, the founder and perfecter of our faith, who for the joy that was set before him endured the cross, despising the shame, and is seated at the right hand of the throne of God (Hebrews 12:1-2).

Jesus had the great wisdom to see beyond the present into the purpose of His death. He could see the joy His sacrifice would bring to all the redeemed. He could see the generations yet unborn who would serve Him. Perhaps He could see the results of millions of lives changed through His sacrifice. He knew being lifted up would draw all men to Him (John 12:32). The joy in heaven over one sinner who repents would be His joy because He paid the price for that sinner's forgiveness.

Perhaps the joy set before Him was the day the redeemed enter the heavenly city. His family washed in His blood will gather to live with Him eternally. What a great homecoming! How happily the Lord will share His glory with His saints (Romans 8:17; 2 Thessalonians 1:10-12). He will supply an abundant entrance into the eternal kingdom (2 Peter 1:10-11). God has a dwelling place for each of His children "so that in the coming ages he might show the immeasurable riches of his grace in kindness toward us in Christ Jesus" (John 14:1-3; Ephesians 2:7). In His pain and humiliation, Jesus could see more.

Let us with resolute heart endure our cross to the end. "But the one who endures to the end will be saved" (Matthew 10:22; 24:13). We may reassure our hearts, as the Lord did to those at Smyrna, "Do not fear what you are about to suffer. Behold, the devil is about to throw some of you into prison, that you may be tested, and for ten days you will have tribulation. Be faithful unto death, and I will give you the crown of life" (Revelation 2:10).

We all need encouragement. I love the inspiring essay "The Fellowship of the Unashamed," [2] which I have adapted below:

I am part of the fellowship of the unashamed. I am strengthened in the Lord and the power of His might. The pattern has been fixed. I have made the decision to call Jesus Lord. I am a disciple and a soldier of Jesus Christ. I am His, body and soul, mind and spirit.

I won't look up, let up, slow down, back away, or be still. There is a world lost in sin, and only the one true gospel can make a difference.

I'm not all I ought to be, what I want to be, or what I am going to be; but, thank God that by His grace, I am not what I used to be. I have no desire to return.

I am finished with low living, sight walking, blind eyes, smooth knees, lazy preaching, deaf ears, compromised beliefs, politically correct talking, and dwarfed goals.

I am finished with giving in to human religion rather than embracing New Testament Christianity. I am weary of scoffers who believe they have something better than God's way or God's will.

I am finished with the notion that the Lord's church has to change its doctrine or it can't grow. I have seen with my eyes that the Gospel still works, the blood still cleanses, God still answers prayers, and the promises of God hold true.

I am finished with foolish ways. I will do more than listen to the Lord; I will carefully obey Him. I will do more than speak for what is right; I will speak against what is wrong. I will do more than hold private beliefs; I will preach the truth without fear to anyone and everyone.

I am finished with doubting. I will believe that every word of every sentence of every verse of every chapter of every book is inspired – God breathed – and is utterly, utterly, utterly trustworthy. I will believe this without apology.

I am finished being wise in my own eyes; I know I do not have a better way. I will not lean on my understanding but will trust God, who knows what I do not know and can see what I cannot see.

I will stand against the compromising of doctrine, the tolerating of human traditions, the offering of false hope, and flirting with popular religion.

I know there is no way to heaven but the narrow way. I am unwilling to endorse any church but the Lord's church, any way but the Lord's way, any gospel but the Lord's gospel, any baptism but the Lord's baptism, or any teaching but the Lord's teaching.

I no longer need preeminence, prosperity, position, promotions, plaudits, or popularity. I have the love of Christ, the grace of God, and the gift of the Holy Spirit.

My pace is set, my gait is fast, my goal is heaven, my road is narrow, my way is rough, my companions few, my guide reliable, and my mission clear.

I must not be bought, compromised, deterred, lured away, turned back, diluted, or delayed. There are too many souls at stake, and my Lord deserves better.

I will not flinch in the face of heresy, hesitate in the presence of error, negotiate at the table of the enemy, pander to the popular, or meander in the maze of the muddy.

I won't give up, back up, let up, or shut up until I have preached up, prayed up, stored up, and stayed up the cause of Christ.

I am a disciple of Jesus Christ. I must go until heaven returns, serve until I drop, preach until everyone knows, and work until He comes. And when He comes to get His own, I pray He'll say, "Well done, good and faithful servant."

Questions

1. In what way is the preaching concerning the cross of Christ an answer to the challenges the church faces today?

2. What does the cross of Christ tell us about our need for repentance?

3. How is the cross of Christ central to the outreach efforts of a congregation?

4. How is a Christian to "take up his cross daily"?

ENDNOTES

Preface
1 Quoted in Daniel S. Udrescu, *Godly Business* (Fairfax, Va.: Xulon Press, 2002) 259.

Chapter 1
1 Johannes P. Louw and Eugene A. Nida, eds., *Greek-English Lexicon of the New Testament Based on Semantic Domains*, 2nd ed. (New York: United Bible Societies, 1989) I:349-365.

2 "Many Americans Say Other Faiths Can Lead to Eternal Life." *The Pew Forum on Religion & Public Life* 18 Dec. 2008. 7 Sept. 2010 <http://pew-forum.org/Many-Americans-Say-Other-Faiths-Can-Lead-to-Eternal-Life.aspx>.

3 Ed Dobson, Wayne Gordon, and Louis McBurney, *Standing Fast: Ministry in an Unfriendly World,* Mastering Ministry's Pressure Points Ser. (Sisters: Multnomah, 1994) S. 34.

Chapter 2
1 For more discussion on this point, see my book *Adrift: Postmodernism in the Church* (Nashville: Gospel Advocate, 2000) 144-148. Chapter 8, "Finding the Map: We Know Where We Are!", also deals with the nature of obedience.

Chapter 3

1   D.A. Carson, *Christ and Culture Revisited* (Grand Rapids, Mich.: Eerdmans, 2008) 11.

2   For a detailed discussion of this subject, see Joseph Fletcher and John Warwick Montgomery, *Situation Ethics: Right or Wrong* (Minneapolis: Dimension Books, 1972).

Chapter 4

1   Allan Bloom, *The Closing of the American Mind* (New York: Simon and Schuster, 1987) 25.

2   Quoted by D.P. Diffine, *One Nation Under God – How Close a Separation?* (Searcy: Harding University, Belden Center for Private Enterprise Education, 6th edition, 1992) 12.

3   "A Barometer of Modern Morals." *Pew Research Center Publications* 28 March 2006. 26 June 2010 <http://pewresearch.org/pubs/307/a-baromeer-of-modern-morals>.

4   "Most Americans believe in the concept of sin, but differ widely on just what it is," *Grey Matter Research & Consulting* 11 March 2008. 29 June 2010 <http://greymatterresearch.com/index_files/Sin.htm>.

5   Chad Hall, "Live Nude God," *Next-Wave Magazine* April 2002. 29 June 2010 <http://www.next-wave.org/apr02/livenudegod.htm>.

6   Letha Scanzoni and Virginia Mollenkott, *Is the Homosexual My Neighbor?* (New York: HarperOne, 1994) 226.

7   Robert Williams, *Just As I Am: A Practical Guide to Being Out, Proud, and Christian* (New York: HarperPerennial, 1993) 128.

8   Phil Sanders, "Today's Taboo (It's Not What You Think It Is)," *Think* December 2007: 11-12.

9   "Sexual Orientation & Homosexuality: Answers to Your Questions for a Better Understanding," *American Psychological Association* 2010. 29 June 2010 <http://www.apa.org/topics/sexuality/orientation.aspx>.

Chapter 5

1   "Jesus Died for 'Climate Change'?" *The Museum of Idolatry* 29 May 2007. 29 June 2010 <http://www.alittleleaven.com/2007/05/booze_for_jesus.html>.

2   Flavil Yeakley Jr., "Where Are the Children?", *Life's Greatest Questions: The 35th Annual Lectureship East Tennessee School of Preaching and Missions* (Knoxville, Tenn.: ETSOP&M, 2009) 162. Longtime researcher

Yeakley of Harding University also noted that when one counts those who return to churches of Christ after marriage and children, the church overall was retaining 67 percent of its children. Yeakley said the churches that were less extreme had the best chance of retaining their children. Those who were extreme to the right also had a difficult time retaining their children (39.9 percent). In contrast, the middle-of-the-road churches kept 62 percent from falling and saw another 12 percent return to active participation.

3 "Faith in Flux: Changes in Religious Affiliation in the United States," *The Pew Forum on Religion & Public Life* 27 April 2009. 1 July 2010 <http://pewforum.org/Faith-in-Flux.aspx>.

4 "Americans Are Exploring New Ways of Experiencing God," *The Barna Group* 8 June 2009. 1 July 2010 <http://www.barna.org/barna-update/article/12-faithspirituality/270-americans-are-exploring-new-ways-of-experiencing-god>.

5 Everett Ferguson, *Baptism in the Early Church* (Grand Rapids, Mich.: Eerdmans, 2009) 64, fn. 27. Ferguson says there are as many as 150 ritual baths in Jerusalem. He cites Ronny Reich, who identified 286 possible ritual baths in Israel.

6 Ken Ham and Britt Beemer with Todd Hillard, *Already Gone: Why Your Kids Will Quit Church and What You Can Do to Stop It* (Green Forest, Ark.: Master Books, 2009) 109-111. Ham notes that teaching and training in matters of faith are what keep young people faithful. The fun, games, style of music and youth group activities did not equip young people to face the faith challenges of our time. He believes that much of what churches do to keep kids is a false relevancy.

7 Ham and Beemer 110.

Chapter 6

1 Thomas A. Helmbock, "Insights on Tolerance," *Cross and Crescent* (a publication of Lambda Chi Alpha International Fraternity), summer 1996: 2. Quoted by Josh McDowell and Bob Hostetler, *The New Tolerance* (Wheaton, Ill.: Tyndale, 1998) 19.

2 Ryan Dobson, *Be Intolerant* (Portland: Multnomah, 2003) 36.

3 Richard H. Schmidt, *God Seekers: Twenty Centuries of Christian Spiritualities* (Grand Rapids, Mich.: Eerdmans, 2008) 281.

4 Jeff Johnson, "Rosie's View: 'Radical Christians' same as 9/11 Terrorists," *Crosswalk.com* 12 Sept. 2006. 8 Sept. 2010 <http://222.crosswalk.com/1424194>.

5   Brad O'Leary, *Shut Up America!: The End of Free Speech* (Los Angeles, Calif.: WND Books, 2009) 103. O'Leary cites Internal Revenue Service code, Rev. Rul. 86-95. IRS Revenue Ruling, published 11 Aug. 1986. 10 Dec. 2010. <http://www.campaignlegalcenter.org/attachments/IRS_PRO-CEEDINGS/1189.pdf>.

6   Joseph Farah, "Repeal the Johnson Amendment," *WorldNetDaily* 25 Feb. 2008. 1 July 2010 <http://wind.com/index.php?fa=PAGE.view&pageId=57224>.

7   David Kinnaman and Gabe Lyons, *Unchristian: What a New Generation Really Thinks About Christianity* (Grand Rapids, Mich.: Baker, 2007) 28.

8   Ravi Zacharias, *Deliver Us from Evil: Restoring the Soul in a Disintegrating Culture* (Dallas: Word, 1996) 114.

9   Adrian Rogers, *The Berean Call* Dec. 1996: 3, 10 Dec. 2010 <http://oakridge church.com/riggs/ph1-27.htm>.

Chapter 7

1   Robert B. Cialdini, *Influence: How and Why People Agree to Things* (New York: William Morrow, 1984) 118. See also Wilson Bryan Key, *The Age of Manipulation* (New York: Henry Holt, 1989).

2   The concept behind this quote, which is universally attributed but never cited in a footnote, comes from Adolf Hitler in his book *Mein Kampf*, trans. Vol. 1, p. 231. Goebbels adapted this quote and probably spoke it privately.

3   Noelle-Neumann, E. (1991). The theory of public opinion: The concept of the Spiral of Silence. In J. A. Anderson (Ed.), Communication Yearbook 14, 256-287. Newbury Park, CA: Sage. For more information on this agenda strategy see Simpson, C. (1996). "Elisabeth Noelle-Neumann's 'spiral of silence' and the historical context of communication theory." Journal of Communication 46 (3):149-173.

4   Peter Fritzsche, *Life and Death in the Third Reich* (Cambridge, Mass.: Belknap Press of Harvard University Press, 2008) 98.

5   "Obama Hopes to Persuade All Americans to Accept Homosexuality," Associated Press, 10 Dec. 2010 <http://www.freerepublic.com/focus/news/2282523/posts>.

Chapter 8

1   J.I. Packer, "Introduction," The Best in Theology (Carol Stream, Ill.: Christianity Today, Inc., 1987) Vol. 1, 17.

2 Stephen D. Renn, ed., *Expository Dictionary of Bible Words* (Peabody, Mass.: Hendrickson Publishers, 2005) 488.

3 Ralph Earle, *Word Meanings in the New Testament* (Peabody, Mass.: Hendrickson Publishers, 1986) 416.

4 William D. Mounce, *Mounce's Complete Expository Dictionary of Old and New Testament Words* (Grand Rapids, Mich.: Zondervan, 2006) 217.

5 Johannes P. Louw and Eugene A. Nida, *Greek-English Lexicon of the New Testament Based on Semantic Domains*, second edition, ed. Rondal B. Smith and Karen A. Munson (New York: United Bible Societies) I:366.

6 J.W. Roberts, "The Letter of James," *The Living Word Commentary*, 178.

7 Wiersbe, Warren W.: *The Bible Exposition Commentary*. (Wheaton, Ill. : Victor Books, 1996, c1989) S. Jas 5:19.

8 Jimmy Jividen, *Koinonia: A Contemporary Study of Church Fellowship* (Nashville: Gospel Advocate, 1989) 99.

9 Jividen 99.

10 Rubel Shelly and John York, *The Jesus Proposal* (Siloam Springs, Ark.: Leafwood Publishers, 2003) 174-175.

11 Elders of University Church of Christ in Las Cruces, N.M., unpublished letter to members, 4 Jan. 2009.

Chapter 9

1 Mark Driscoll, from a lecture on The Emerging Church Movement at the Southern Baptist Theological Seminary, Sept. 22, 2007 <http://emerging-churchconcerns.wordpress.com/part-iv-conclusions-and-recommendations/ accessed 8/27/2010>.

2 Tony Jones, from a lecture at the 2005 National Youth Workers Convention <http://www.omegatimes.com/article.php?intid=1289>.

3 Kim Lawton, interviewed for "The Emerging Church, Part One," Religion & Ethics Newsweekly, July 8, 2005, <http://www.pbs.org/wnet/religion-andethics/week845/cover.html> accessed 8/27/2010.

4 Brian McLaren, see Kim Lawton above.

5 Peter F. Drucker, *Post-Capitalist Society* (New York: Harper Paperbacks, 1994) 1.

6 Mark Driscoll, "Navigating the Emerging Church Highway," *Christian Research Journal*, April 2008: 11-21.

7 Driscoll 15.

8 Brian McLaren, *The Church on the Other Side* (Grand Rapids, Mich.: Zondervan, 2000) 14-15.

9 Brian McLaren, *A Generous Orthodoxy* (Grand Rapids, Mich.: Zondervan, 2006) 260, 262, 264.

10 McLaren, *Generous* 264.

11 Brian McLaren, "Ramadan 2009: Part 3," August 17, 2009 <http://www.brianmclaren.net/archives/2009/08/>.

12 Neil Livingstone, "How Can You Trust the Bible?" 10 <http://chitv.org/ourprograms/Adult%20Classes/The%20Story/howcanyoutrustthebible%5B1%5D.pdf>.

13 Stanley Hauerwas, *Unleashing the Scripture: Freeing the Bible from Captivity to America* (Nashville: Abingdon, 1993) 17.

14 Alan Jones, *Reimagining Christianity* (Hoboken: John Wiley & Sons, 2005) 79, 83.

15 Driscoll 18.

16 McLaren said this in a lecture at the Festival of Homiletics in Nashville, Tenn., May 2007.

17 *ApologeticsIndex*, 22 Sept. 2010 <http://www.apologeticsindex.org/303-emerging-church-versus-doctrine>.

18 *ApologeticsIndex*.

19 Robert E. Klenck, video titled, "Diaprax and the Church: Manipulating the Church into Globalism."

Chapter 11

1 Charles Spurgeon, *The Quotable Spurgeon* (Wheaton, Ill.: Harold Shaw Publishers, Inc., 1990), n.p.

2 John C. Maxwell, *How Successful People Think* (New York: Center Street, 2007) 83.

3 Maxwell, 82-83.

4 Henry, Matthew: *Matthew Henry's Commentary on the Whole Bible: Complete and Unabridged in One Volume* (Peabody: Hendrickson, 1996, c1991) S. Matthew 7:13-14.

Chapter 12

1 Many things in this chapter were originally delivered as a lecture in the 35th Annual Lectureship at the East Tennessee School of Preaching and Missions. See Phil Sanders, "Who Is My Brother?" in *Life's Greatest Questions* (Knoxville, Tenn.: ETSOP&M, 2009) 295-303.

2 Shelly and York 171-175.

3 Quotations in this section come from the Great Communion website found at <http://greatcommunion.org/about.htm>.

4 For a detailed study, see J.E. Choate and William Woodson, *Sounding Brass and Clanging Cymbals: The History and Significance of Instrumental Music in the Restoration Movement 1827-1968* (Henderson: Freed-Hardeman University Press, 1990) 161-205.

Chapter 13

1 The inference for this comes from Acts 26:10: "And I did so in Jerusalem. I not only locked up many of the saints in prison after receiving authority from the chief priests, but when they were put to death I cast my vote against them."

2 Some attribute the original "The Fellowship of the Unashamed" essay to Dr. Bob Moorehead and others to Henry B. Eyring. The original source remains unknown.